T0318844

Cambridge Elements ≡

Elements in Religion and Violence
edited by
James R. Lewis
University of Tromsø
Margo Kitts
Hawai'i Pacific University

RELIGIOUS CULTURE AND VIOLENCE IN TRADITIONAL CHINA

Barend ter Haar
University of Hamburg

CAMBRIDGE
UNIVERSITY PRESS

CAMBRIDGE
UNIVERSITY PRESS

University Printing House, Cambridge CB2 8BS, United Kingdom

One Liberty Plaza, 20th Floor, New York, NY 10006, USA

477 Williamstown Road, Port Melbourne, VIC 3207, Australia

314–321, 3rd Floor, Plot 3, Splendor Forum, Jasola District Centre,
New Delhi – 110025, India

79 Anson Road, #06–04/06, Singapore 079906

Cambridge University Press is part of the University of Cambridge.

It furthers the University's mission by disseminating knowledge in the pursuit of
education, learning, and research at the highest international levels of excellence.

www.cambridge.org
Information on this title: www.cambridge.org/9781108706230
DOI: 10.1017/9781108613392

First published 2019

A catalogue record for this publication is available from the British Library.

ISBN 978-1-108-70623-0 Paperback
ISSN: 2397-9496 (online)
ISSN: 2514-3786 (print)

Religious Culture and Violence in Traditional China

Elements in Religion and Violence

DOI: 10.1017/9781108613392

First published online: May 2019

Barend ter Haar

University of Hamburg

Author for correspondence: Barend ter Haar, barend.ter.haar@uni-hamburg.de

ABSTRACT: The basis of Chinese religious culture, and with that many aspects of daily life, was the threat and fear of demonic attacks. These were inherently violent and could only be counteracted by violence as well – even if this reactive violence was masked by euphemisms such as execution, expulsion, exorcisms and so on. At the same time, violence was a crucial dimension of the maintenance of norms and values, for instance in sworn agreements or in beliefs about underworld punishment. Violence was also an essential aspect of expressing respect through sacrificial gifts of meat (and in an earlier stage of Chinese culture also human flesh) and through a culture of auto-mutilation and ritual suicide. At the same time conventional indigenous terms for violence such as bao 暴 were not used for most of these practices, since they were not experienced as such, but were justified as positive uses of physical force.

KEYWORDS: sacred, revenge, Oceania, violence, reciprocity, warfare

ISBNs: 9781108706230 (PB), 9781108613392 (OC)

ISSNs: 2397-9496 (online), 2514-3786 (print)

Contents

Preface

This Element reflects the limitations of my knowledge and the extent of my hubris in tackling the huge topic of violence and religious culture in traditional China. Since there is not really a systematic field of study in many of the topics discussed in what follows, oftentimes my conclusions can only be tentative. The annotations are indicative and not exhaustive, leaving out most of the empirical evidence and much scholarly evaluation. I have generally given only Western language references, since this Element is intended for a relatively broad audience that does not necessarily read Chinese or Japanese. I want to thank Yves Menheere, Mark Meulenbeld and Margot Kitts for reading earlier versions. I am especially grateful to the editors of this series for the opportunity to develop my ideas further, in more detail and more systematically than in earlier articles or book fragments.

A Selective Historical Periodization

Shang 商	ca. 1550–ca. 1045 BCE
Zhou 周	ca. 1045–256 BCE
Qin 秦	221–206 BCE
Han 漢	202 BCE–9 CE and 25–220
Xin 新	9–23
Period of Disunion	221–589
Sui 隋	589–618
Tang 唐	618–907
Period of Five Dynasties	907–960
Northern Song 宋	960–1127
Southern Song	1127–1276
Jin (Jurchen; northern China) 金	1115–1234
Yuan (Mongols) 元	1272–1368
Ming 明	1368–1644
Qing (Manchus) 清	1644–1911
Republic of China 中華民國	1912–present (since 1949 on Taiwan)
People's Republic of China 中華人民共和國	1949–present

Setting the Stage

This Element deals with very sensitive issues, so it is important to begin with several caveats. The term 'violence' is very much a normative term for forms of physical force that we disapprove of. Therefore not every reader will agree with the broad use of the term in the cultural analysis that follows. I certainly do not wish to claim that traditional China was more, or less, violent than other cultures, including Western European ones. Since the term is so difficult to quantify without making all kinds of normative assumptions and Chinese historical sources are often spotty on this topic, I also do not see how this kind of comparison would be possible. What I do wish to claim is that different forms of violence played an important role in Chinese religious culture. In this Element I provide a summary discussion of the contexts within which we find such violence, which can hopefully serve as a basis for further discussion and polemics.

Like any other culture, we talk about China in terms and categories derived from the dominant elite discourse, and more specifically the written and normative variant of this discourse. It is surprisingly difficult to escape this discourse and create an independent way of looking at various aspects of Chinese culture (see also Murphy, 2011; Soboslai, 2015). The history of violence is not fundamentally different in this respect, as we see in what follows. We therefore need to pay special attention to the question what is included or excluded within this history: an example is the exclusion of blood vengeance. Early writers believed that it was sanctioned by Confucius himself, hence not to be considered violence. When such vengeance was gradually seen as deviance from the eleventh century onwards, the text which quoted Confucius' permission was largely forgotten in the process. Or take the general exclusion from Chinese history writing of the genocidal repression of local ethnic groups ('minorities'), even when thousands of people were killed, for instance in the campaigns in the early sixteenth century by the famous neo-Confucian philosopher Wang Yangming 王陽明 (1472–1529). Instead, China is preferably seen by Western historians as a place in which *wen* 文 or 'pattern' dominates and in which society strives for harmony in human relationships. The Chinese term is then further analysed as written culture, civilization or otherwise.

That these 'patterns' are based on violence, without which political order and social hierarchy cannot be enforced, is generally overlooked (ter Haar, 2000). The notion of *wen* forms part of a conceptual pair, together with *wu* 武 or martial (i.e. good) violence, which still excludes many forms of what could well be considered violence such as domestic abuse, torture and the death penalty.

What people see as violence therefore varies considerably among different cultures, as well as different periods of time, social groups, educational levels, gender, and age groups – to mention only a few possibilities. Even when I limit myself to the different societies in which I have grown up and subsequently spent much of my working life, our understanding of 'violence' has evolved considerably, meaning that we now think some forms of behaviour are 'obviously' violent and others are legitimate. And this is quite apart from the fact that as an individual I might have (and have had) different views from the rest of this large group, and from myself in the past and who knows in the future. A simple example of recent change is the conscious and 'reasoned' use of physical force in raising children, such as a slap on the buttocks, hands or face, which was once considered acceptable and is now essentially forbidden. An example of biased perspective is that of terror and counterterror. While terrorists are considered by us to be 'obviously' violent, we tend to use euphemisms or less pejorative terms for the fight against terror and rarely label our efforts as violent as well. To us, almost any form of counteraction using physical force is defined as war ('the war on terror') and the thousands of victims who fall in this war (far more than through terrorist attacks) are defined as war deaths (if they are combatants) or even executions (if they are defined as terrorists), and the huge number of civilian victims as collateral damage.

This Element is devoted to the role of violence in traditional Chinese religious culture, with violence in the sense of real or imagined physical force, with words like 'real' and 'imagined' as our modern labels for what people at the time often did not separate in the same way. The most obvious equivalent for 'violence' in Chinese would be the term *bao* 暴. If we limited ourselves to those instances in which something is pejoratively labelled as such, we would have a very different discussion. Here I make the choice of vocabulary an important part of our discussion, but otherwise adopt a very broad view of what could be included under the label of violence as a general analytical concept, rather than as the translation of the normative concept of *bao* or 'violence'. This creates a certain tension, since it means imposing my view, my categorizations and my connections between phenomena in ways that people from the regions and periods that I am studying would not have agreed with. Although this is true of most research, the discrepancy between my categories and those of the past feels more jarring with sensitive topics such as violence. For this reason I retain parts of the original Chinese language discourse, even though this is meant to be an introductory work for a broad readership. This should allow readers with some knowledge of Chinese to test my judgement against their own.

Another problem term is 'religion'. As the reader may have noticed, I use the term 'religious culture', rather than religion. I do so because traditional China did not have a separate sphere of religion, but large parts of political, legal, social, cultural and sometimes even economic life did entail activities that we would today call religious (Goossaert and Palmer, 2011). Thus, to investigate religion in traditional China is to single out the religious dimension of that period, which extends from the imperial institution to the formation of local institutions such as the family (through ancestor worship) and the village (through local cults). In order to understand this dimension, one cannot avoid touching upon the non-religious dimensions as well. Since this is just an introduction I do not provide further discussion of this and similar problem words here, such as the term 'politics' (Lagerwey, 2010), but pretend that there is some common ground between the author and the readers.

In my analysis, traditional China was a place filled with violence, not much less than for instance Western society for most of its history (compare however Pinker, 2011). Whether Chinese at the time would have described it with the same terminology is another matter. There was the death penalty in its various guises, usually including the display of the corpse or at least the head of the executed person. Torture was used on witnesses and suspects during legal procedures, in order to obtain what was seen as reliable evidence in a time and age without forensic science. Physical punishment and maltreatment happened regularly within any hierarchical relationship, such as education at home and in school, within a marriage and in the household or between a landowner and his labourers. Some of this would have been seen as appropriate, although there was also a discourse that criticized the unjust use of violence in exploitation. The deity Lord Guan (or Guan Yu 關羽) was famously known for his killing of a local bully who was kidnapping local women. Whether people actually did use violence in such situations is another matter, but clearly there was some measure of support for Lord Guan's violence in the service of local justice on a narrative level. After all, he was one of the most popular deities in late imperial China and versions of this story were told in the north for many centuries (ter Haar, 2017).

Physical force was an essential element of local religious culture. Indeed, Lord Guan himself as a deity was well known for threatening with, and sometimes using, violence to protect local communities and individual people. Nonetheless, this was never labelled as *bao* ('violence') but as punishment. We might even label it as symbolic, and therefore less threatening to our own cultural values. The following case took place in the early twelfth century, when a county in northern China was plagued by a white snake (Hong, 1981: *zhixu* 9: 1119–20). The situation escalated to the point that the Song emperor sent one of his leading Daoist priests to address the problem. This was the Heavenly Master Zhang Jixian 張濟先 (1092–1127), a major figure in Daoist ritual tradition. He summoned the local deities to tell him where the creature was, but not even the City God dared to reveal its whereabouts. Zhang became angry and sharply rebuked him. 'He commanded spirit soldiers to wield sticks and whips, causing extreme pain.' Under this punitive violence, the City God revealed that the white snake was well connected with Heaven and therefore beyond his control. The Heavenly Master threatened him that he would be executed (*lu* 戮) if he did not reveal the location of the snake. Thereupon the Master had a huge platform built near the nest, making the complete population of the city stand on it and having his assistants carry out rituals.

First, the Heavenly Master made the creature appear with the help of coloured amulets. A fierce white vapour (*baiqi* 白氣) manifested itself from the sky and everybody on the platform was afraid of being swallowed alive. The Master instructed them to take some of the earth of the platform in their mouths for protection. Thereupon he had the seal of the prefecture placed before him as a sign of authority and challenged the vapour to show itself in its full form. A huge white snake appeared, but the Master was able to control it with his seal and killed it (*sha* 殺) with a flying sword. Small snakes appeared continuously, so he had to think of a more practical solution. Using his ritual powers he tied down the creatures and with the knives and swords of the local leaders he executed (*zhu* 誅) the biggest by beheading (*zhan* 斬). The rest were handed over to divine generals (*shen-jiang* 神將) to be driven out (*quchu* 驅出) of the territory. When they inspected the nest of the snakes, it was filled with the pale bones of their victims.

It would be too easy to dismiss this account as fictional, since for people at the time, on all levels of society, it was entirely plausible. There are many similar accounts in which a ritual specialist uses physical force of some kind to expel a demonic and often violent threat. This force is described with the same words that one finds in real-life legal practice or military campaigns. None of the Chinese verbs for killing or punishment in this account refers to 'violence' or *bao* 暴 as a random occurrence of physical force. The brutal behaviour of the exorcist against the City God as well as the demonic snakes was no different from that of the local magistrate towards his usual suspects in a murder trial or local revolt. Killing (*sha*), executing (*lu*, *zhu*) and beheading (*zhan*) were commonly accepted ways of dealing with real-life rebels and murderers. This elaborate exorcism was directly modelled on real-life events, although people witnessed such ritual executions much more often than real-life ones. Especially after these events had been turned into narratives for further transmission, they became as real as ordinary executions of living human beings. Quite possibly, they helped shape people's perceptions of real-life executions as much as the other way around.

There is much that is not discussed in this Element, not so much because it is not important, but mostly because of a lack of space. One such topic is the use of religious practices surrounding war and other forms of collective fighting, such as banditry or rebellions (Waley-Cohen, 2006; Katz, 2009b; McMullen, 1989). Sometimes religious practices were used to cover up very real human violence, for instance the many stories of deities who rape women which mostly likely reflected rapes by close kin or neighbours that could only be given therapeutic narrative form as divine or demonic rapes (Von Glahn, 2004b). Excluded are also various martial arts traditions, which we know best in their Buddhist form of the Shaolin tradition, but which also had Daoist forms (Shahar, 2008). I also leave out Confucian-inspired forms of violence, although the early advocacy of blood vengeance ascribed to Confucius or the ideologically motivated protest suicides of the late imperial period would certainly qualify (Wyatt, 2011; Burton-Rose, 2018).

What Is Violence?

Perceptions of what counted as good or bad violence changed over time (ter Haar, 2000). The most common term for transgressive violence in Chinese is *bao* 暴. The relevant entry for this term in the encyclopaedic *Great Dictionary of the Chinese Language* provides a wealth of examples, ranging from its explicit denotations of excessive cruelty, coercing people in inferior positions, harming and damaging, or violent rebellion, to derivative meanings such as abrupt, sudden or fierce. Pronounced as *pu*, the same character means to expose oneself to the scorching sun as a sacrifice in exchange for rain (Luo, 1986: vol. V, 827–31). This range of meanings remains fairly standard from the oldest transmitted texts onwards until the present, both in formal prose and poetry and in vernacular literature. To my knowledge one of the few people who have analysed the term in any depth is Virgil Ho. He argues that the term 'violence' in its Anglo-Saxon usage does not map well onto Chinese conceptions. According to him, the term *bao* in traditional China cannot be simply equated with the modern term *baoli* 暴力 that roughly translates the term 'violence' (Ho, 2000: 141–5). In my view it does mean inappropriate violence, in traditional China as well as today. The real problem is that what was thought of as inappropriate changed considerably over time.

The term *bao* was foundational to notions of good and bad government. Thus, an early history from around 100 BCE already tells us that:

> [W]hen the age of the Divine Farmer (*shennong* 神農) went into decline, the feudal lords started to fight each other. They were violent and cruel (*baonüe* 暴虐) towards the hundred family names. The Divine Farmer was unable to

punish them. Thereupon the Yellow Emperor practised the use of weapons in order to punish those who would not submit. The feudal lords all came to subordinate themselves and follow him. Chiyou was the most violent (*bao*) of them all, but none could subjugate him.
(Sima, 1959: 1: 3)

The Yellow Emperor would succeed in smiting Chiyou, dispersing his body parts across the northern plains, with his inner organs forming the red salt ponds of Xie. The precise nature of Chiyou's 'violence' is not specified, but there can be little doubt that he received the most gruesome fate of all. Because the destruction of his body was perpetrated by the Yellow Emperor in the service of the forces of order, it was not seen as 'violence' or *bao*, but as subjugation (*fa* 伐 or *ping* 平) (ter Haar, 2017: 70–1). All later human rulers would maintain the same distinction between bad or random violence (*bao*) and sanctioned violence, for which a whole range of euphemisms existed.

In 221 BCE the Qin dynasty created the first unified empire that we now see as the territorial ancestor of China today. It was the end result of centuries of warfare. Violence was an important part of its rule, through harsh (but consistent) punishment and military repression. During his reign, the First Emperor made several long trips to important mountain sites all over his empire. Here he worshipped Heaven and Earth, but the whole enterprise of these large-scale trips also served to make his imperial rule visible over the All-under-Heaven as Chinese called the civilized world that they knew. On the mountains he had stones erected with inscriptions in an archaic form of the classical written language (Kern, 2000). The texts emphasized the order brought by the Qin unification. Whereas traditional historiography has stereotyped his reign as violent and cruel, the inscriptions claim the reverse.

'The feudal lords each guarded their own territories ...
They invaded each other and engaged in violence and chaos.' 'The August Thearch had pity on the masses and thereupon he dispatched his punitive army and wielded his martial virtue ... He boiled and destroyed those who were strong and violent, and he rescued the ordinary people.'

'With martial means he exterminated the violent and rebellious.' 'Internal forces dressed up with deceitful plotting and
external forces came to invade the borders, thereby causing
disasters and catastrophes. With righteous might we executed them, to eliminate the violent and rebellious'
(Sima, 1959: 6: 246, 249–50, 252, 261).

The Qin dynasty used righteous might and martial means, in other words
a devastating war, to remove the random violence (*bao*) of the feudal lords.

Whether we agree with the view presented by the Qin inscriptions is
beyond the point. The term 'violence' (*bao*) is clearly used in the same
normative way as by us today. As the language of the inscriptions shows,
suppressing 'violence' required 'pacification and settling down' (*pingding*
平定), by means of execution, elimination, destruction and extermination.
Later rulers and their generals would act no differently. When the neo-
Confucian philosopher Wang Yangming (1472–1529) served as an official
to repress a rebellion (as he saw it) by the Yao ethnicity in southern Jiangxi,
he had no qualms in using what we would now see as genocidal violence. He
is also one of the most important philosophers of later imperial history,
basing his philosophical thought on the notion that everybody possesses an
innate consciousness of what it entails to do good. This should then
translate into the proper form of action in any given situation. During the
suppression of the Yao people, he executed many thousands of people in
addition to the usual victims during battle itself (Israel, 2014: 279–313). At
no point was this seen as 'violence' (*bao*) by him or later writers but merely
as the legitimate application of force.

It seems to me that the use of violence was not just a matter of establish-
ing control and order, if necessary by the extermination of the perceived
causes of disorder, but also a powerful means of communication. Put very
simply, violence speaks strongly and for this reason the reality of violence
was central to its appearance in all dimensions of life, including religious
culture. Ritual practice, exorcist theatre and festival processions gave concrete form to the punitive violence with which demons could be exorcised
and punished. People who received a supernatural punishment often died
very visibly, such as by lightning, or they suffered debilitating illnesses

which showed them in excessive pain and uncontrolled trembling, with disfigured skin and body.[1] Violence was also a public and easy-to-understand display of power.

The presentation of a living being to supernatural forces, in early days also humans and until today a variety of animals, was not symbolic, but a real sacrifice due to the violence of killing. By sharing the meat with the deities in the case of animal sacrifice, a potent bond was created between the supernatural forces and all those who participated in the offering. Therefore good or sanctioned violence was not seen as 'violence (*bao*)' (Lewis, 1990). Historically, the principal counter-discourse came not so much from the intellectual traditions we nowadays classify as Confucianism or Classicism, which because of their reliance on classical texts were somehow associated with the figure of Confucius (551–479 BCE). These traditions were by no means averse to violence, sacrificial, punitive or otherwise. Instead, the main challenge came from Buddhism with its injunction against killing, although this did not mean a complete abstention from violence as a language or even the practice of self-sacrifice.

Since what happens in the supernatural world in its various forms is less obviously visible, it is perhaps only natural that the violence in these other worlds is more extreme. Claims about that world needed to be made more strongly to have the requisite effect. The world of the living is used as a source of inspiration, and the supernatural world can be used to reflect on the former, but is still considered just as real. The extreme nature of the violence maybe makes it even more real and more tangible, thanks to such human abilities as empathy and imagination. Jérôme Bourgon has argued for instance that real-life executions were very different from those in the religious world, and this is true to a certain extent (Bourgon, 2003). Nonetheless, Virgil Ho has provided considerable evidence suggesting that the two were still intimately connected. Before their execution the convicts were dehumanized by bad treatment and neglect, making them look more akin to hungry ghosts than humans, and this process continued

---

[1] The term 'supernatural' is not ideal here, since in the eyes of most Chinese at the time the supernatural was only too real. In this Element I use the term as a shortcut for other realms of being than the conventional human world.

after their executions. The magistrate and his assistants might be marked by red clothes, the colour of life and the opposite of the dehumanized appearance of the convicts. The actual executions took place outside the growing season, ideally in winter, but also at a time of day when the sun was strong, with the life force of the sun compensating for the taking of life (Ho, 2000). We have ample occasion in what follows to investigate the importance of underworld justice, which was extremely violent, with the City God behaving much like a magistrate. Whereas one might never encounter a magistrate in real life, one was bound to encounter the City God at various points in one's life and after death.

The Demonological Substrate

The world in which the Chinese lived and worked was filled with a variety of demonic creatures, often of a violent nature. These demons caused all kinds of disturbances, hauntings, illnesses and so forth (good survey in Von Glahn, 2004b). Violence played a crucial role in dealing with this constant onslaught by demons, something that J. J. M. de Groot already called 'the war against spectres' in his description of local religious culture in 1880s Fujian (de Groot, 1901: 928–1185). The outcome of this war was a form of order (*zhi* 治), as the opposite of 'chaos' (*luan* 亂). When similar demons were enlisted as a force to support a larger moral order, they came to be seen as divine beings. Demons might be the ghosts of humans who had died and were lingering on, but also the 'essences' (*jing* 精, a pejorative term) of trees, rocks and other objects (*wu* 物) who had imbibed the energy (*qi* 氣) of the cosmos, and a variety of animalistic monsters whose origin is not always clear, such as the aforementioned Chiyou. The earliest written sources on oracle bones and bronzes are not very informative on this dimension of Chinese culture, but excavated manuscripts from the late third century BCE and after have confirmed its importance (Harper, 1998: 69, 152). From the imperial period onwards, we then have an increasing amount of detail on the rituals and festivals to keep these demons and influences at bay, as well as narrative accounts of concrete cases of demonic attacks and the fight against them (Harper, 1998; Poo, 1998; Bodde, 1975). Medical recipes found in an early second century BCE grave include a wealth of exorcist approaches. One recipe goes as follows, in the translation by Donald Harper:

> For lying prostrate. On the sixteenth day of the month when the moon first begins to deteriorate, perform the Pace of Yu thrice. Say: 'Moon is matched against sun' and 'Sun is matched against moon' – three times each. 'Father is perverse, Mother is strong. Like other people they bore Sons, and only bore inguinal swelling bulges. Perverseness desist. Grasp the hammering stone and strike your Mother.' Immediately exorcistically beat and hammer the person twice seven times with an iron mallet. Do it at sunrise, and have the person with inguinal swelling face east.
> (Harper, 1998: 161–2 with minor changes)

The Pace of Yu is a ritual dance that mimics the walking of the lame ancient king Yu 禹, which would become an important part of Daoist ritual in subsequent centuries. The recipe places the healing ritual in a lunar calendrical context, possibly to profit from larger cosmic energies. The demon causing the ailment is removed with considerable violence (Harper, 1998: 261–2, 291–2, 293–4, 302). King Yu was the one who created the ultimate order in Chinese cosmology, when he rearranged the All-under-Heaven after great floods. The enactment of this ordering process continues to be practised within Daoist ritual until this very day (Lagerwey, 1987).

In the anecdotal record we encounter scores of stories about demons and other anomalous creatures haunting houses and other locations, causing illness and psychic disorder through possession, throwing things around, stealing and so forth. Only suitable counter-violence was capable of dealing with these forms of misbehaviour. A text from circa 300 CE tells the story of someone who was able to 'indict' (*he* 劾) the 'hundred ghosts and masses of demons' (*baigui zhongmei* 百鬼眾魅).

> A woman from his region was made ill by a demon (*mei* 魅). He indicted it for her and they got a big snake of several fathoms dead in front of her door. The woman regained her

peace thanks to this. There was also a big tree with an
'essence' (*jing*) in it. People who stopped below it would
die. Birds that flew over it would also drop from the sky. He
indicted it and the tree withered in full summer. A big snake
of seven or eight fathoms long hung dead from the tree.
(Gan, 1979: 2: 20)

The emperor then tested his abilities with several fake demons, each time
resulting in the death of these imposters (and their resuscitation at the
request of the emperor). Precisely what kind of ritual this man performed
beyond the 'impeachment' is unclear.

To give a demon its right desert usually required some ritual assistance.
A story set in 806 CE in Raozhou (modern Jiangxi) features the daughter of
the local prefect. She was about to give birth in a back hall of the prefectural
offices, but was pestered in her dreams by a demon or deity who complained
about her 'stench and pollution' (*xinghui* 腥穢) and scolded her to go away.
During labour she was attacked by the demon and died of bleeding from her
ears and nose. The following year, her husband returned home from the
examinations in the capital. He interrogated the local deities why they had
not prevented his wife from being killed by 'violent demons' (*baogui* 暴鬼).
After a formal lawsuit about this case (no doubt with the assistance of ritual
specialists), it was discovered that the demon had been Wu Rui 吳芮,
a former local official who had died of an illness in 202 BCE during the civil
war which had brought the Han dynasty to power. 'He had been angry
about the stench and pollution of her giving birth, and had then committed
random violence (*sixiong bao* 肆凶暴). Thereupon they captured (*qin* 擒)
Wu Rui, submitted a memorial to the Offices of Heaven and executed him'
(Li, 1981: 44: 274–5). The story has clear Daoist overtones in the ritual use
of bureaucratic procedures, but important for us is that the pregnant woman
had died in labour as a result of the violent behaviour of a local demon. This
demon was then executed. This type of exorcism in order to deal with
demons causing death, illness, natural disasters and so forth would be the
stock-in-trade of ritual specialists throughout the following centuries.

Then like now, death meant a disruption of social and familial bonds,
which then had to be reconstituted anew. Dead people were deemed

a potential threat, whether they were within the family or outsiders. One way of dealing with this kind of disruption was the performance of funerary rituals in order to realign the group. In the case of adult males with male progeny, ancestor worship then served to maintain the group over time and space. These rituals of group creation have understandably received much scholarly attention, but there has been much less interest in the disruptive side of death (Faure, 2007). After all, only adults with some descendants or surviving relatives who died at home were likely to receive proper funerary rituals. Many died without such rituals and their extant energy (*qi* 氣) was thought to be highly dangerous. People who died in battle, but also women who died in labour, the victims of mass epidemics and natural disasters and small children who sometimes wasted away within a single day were all potentially violent demons who preyed on the living (Nickerson, 2002).

The violence of the rupture of death was concretized by the ancient belief that the soul of the deceased was collected after passing away by a birdlike creature with sharp claws and a pointed beak. This creature is already documented by the first century CE and was called *sha* 煞 (killer demon), *yang* 殃 (disaster) or *sheng* 眚 (affliction) in the written literature (ter Haar, 2006: 209–12). These names already indicate its violent nature. The soul was thought to return one more time to the corpse within a few days after its demise, accompanied by this creature (Sawada, 1982). This visit was considered highly dangerous and rituals were performed to prevent anything serious from happening. According to an early nine-teenth-century source, an old man in Taicang, who was accomplished in the martial arts, had just lost his son. On the day of the return of the *sheng*, he and a group of friends gathered to try and steal the son back from the deity. When a huge bird with a human face entered the room, the old man stuck his spear into its back. He struggled to hold it, but the bird flapped around vehemently, beating people with its wings. All the old man's friends fell to the ground and when he eventually also tired, the bird succeeded in escaping. The old man's face was entirely blue-green from the beatings, and the faces of his friends also all had a blue-green mark (*qingyin* 青印) on them. This combat is narrated in extremely concrete and realistic terms, including descriptions of the severe bruises inflicted by the demon

(Qian, 1982: 15: 396; also Sawada, 1982: 425, 444). The violent and danger-ous aspect of the freshly deceased person was transferred to the bird and only after it had returned one last time could the deceased cross over to the status of ancestor or at least be reborn (after the advent of Buddhism).

The anecdotal literature from the late imperial period contains many examples of zombies, who were usually people whose body had not yet been put to rest in the ground. Their corpses had been temporarily disposed of in coffins and placed in a religious institution for safekeeping. Such 'stiff corpses' sometimes came alive to haunt the living (Sawada, 1990: 261–89). The eminent late Qing scholar Yu Yue records the case of a young woman who had been killed by her parents because she had a sexual liaison before she was married. They buried her corpse somewhere in the wild. She turned into a zombie and began to harm people. Thereupon they dug up her corpse and cremated it, but the ashes escaped into the sky and people saw a red magpie. Her ghost started to cause harm again, resulting in the death of virtuous maidens. The violence was not directed just at life, but more specifically at the moral order. Nothing helped and even the building of a temple for her did not resolve the threat, which continued for several decades. A local magistrate burned her temple and people asked the Heavenly Master for amulets, which finally provided some relief (Yu, 1986: 5: 128–9). The case was a typical example of someone who had been murdered and buried without ritual. Burning the corpse was quite common in dealing with such zombies.

From the late Han dynasty onwards people increasingly worshipped some of these violently deceased in expectation of their help, rather than just being afraid of them and driving them away. One well-documented exam-ple is that of Jiang Ziwen 蔣子文, a sheriff stationed in modern Nanjing and best known for his dissolute behaviour. Following his violent death at the hands of local bandits, he was seen riding a white horse (a symbol of contact with heaven) and claiming that he should be worshipped as a local deity. After he brought epidemics, deadly ear bugs, and fire disasters (in what was a city mostly built from wood), people finally started to worship him and the disasters stopped (Gan, 1979: 5: 57–61; Lin, 1998). Daoist writers often inveighed against the trend of worshipping these generals, whom they pejoratively described as 'stale energies' (*guqi* 古氣), but eventually they became a very common type of deity, at least in southern China below the Yangzi River (Stein, 1979). Even Lord Guan, who would eventually come to be seen as the epitome of loyalty and righteousness, was still very much a violent deity. Originally, he was merely a fierce and untamed deity on a mountain or a plague-bringing demon, but eventually his physical force was labelled as 'martial' (*wu*) or good violence. He used his force amongst others to protect against bandits and rebels, whether by merely manifesting himself or by actually driving them away (ter Haar, 2017: 21–46). Deities such as Lord Guan would be assisted by their own supernatural armies (Von Glahn, 2004b: 63–4; ter Haar, 2017: 24, 31, 68, 84, 95, 127–9, 170, 176, 200).

The best-known antecedent of such an army is undoubtedly the famous terracotta army of the First Emperor of the Qin, and its smaller versions in the graves of the emperors of the Western Han dynasty. Interesting, the belief also surfaces in connection with the oldest attested religious movement in Chinese history, the Way of the Heavenly Masters, which was then also known as the Five Pecks of Rice. It first manifested itself with a rebellion in 184 CE and occupied the economic core of the modern province of Sichuan. We have already encountered several ritual specialists who claimed to stand in the tradition of these Heavenly Masters. The movement divided its territory into twenty-four *zhi* 治, using the same term for 'ordering' discussed earlier. We usually translate the term here as diocese, but this obscures the semantic connections. Initiated members of the movement were called Demon Soldiers (*guibing* 鬼兵) or Demon Troopers (*guizu* 鬼卒), and controlled a host of further Demon Soldiers to protect them against demonic attacks (Kleeman, 1998: 69, 71 and Kleeman, 2016: 53–5, 177). During a rebellion in the early fifth century, a prominent Daoist believer enlisted the help of 'several Demon Soldiers of the Great Way' (Kleeman, 1998: 69 slightly different). I return to the Heavenly Masters later in this Element, in the context of indigenous messianic movements.

The belief in divine armies that protected against demonic attacks was basic to exorcist ritual practice, but also shaped people's beliefs about their local deities. The early anecdotal literature on divine armies bears abundant witness to these armies, calling them 'Divine Soldiers' (*shenbing* 神兵),

'Heavenly Soldiers' (*tianbing* 天兵), 'Ghost Soldiers' (*yinbing* 陰兵) or even 'Demon Soldiers' (*guibing* 鬼兵). An official who had died in exile was granted permission by the Supreme Thearch (*shangdi* 上帝, not then a term for the Christian God) to enlist 'Ghost Soldiers' to avenge himself on his political enemy and get him killed (Li, 1981: 123: 869; other examples 19: 131: 154: 1105; 290: 2309; 297: 2363–4; 300: 2386; 305: 2414; 306: 2423–4; 321: 2542–3; 375: 2980–1). The evidence from the later imperial period is even more abundant.

Daoist ritual texts likewise regularly refer to Heavenly Soldiers and Divine Soldiers in the service of the ritual specialist, as well as Demon Soldiers and Ghost Soldiers with a more ambivalent or sometimes evil status. They describe massive supernatural battles in great detail, including the violence of war. Later vernacular novels and theatrical plays develop their basic plot structures out of these beliefs and ritual practices (Meulenbeld, 2015; ter Haar, 2017: 127–39). In the following story from an early fourth-century source, a man by the name of Liu Ping 劉憑 successfully practised various techniques to obtain a long life. When merchants heard that he possessed the Way, they asked for his protection on their journey. When they were attacked by bandits, Liu Ping duly enlisted Heavenly Soldiers to destroy them. He used a similar technique of commanding (*chi* 勑) such soldiers against demons that were possessing a woman and even to kill a murderous snake. Finally, he used amulets to kill actors who had been ordered by the emperor to dress up as demons. Only when the emperor admitted that they were not real did Ping make them come alive again (Li, 1981: 11: 74–5; more examples 24: 161–2; 44: 275–6; 285: 2272–3; 453: 3701–4).

By the Northern Song dynasty the evidence in anecdotal collections as well as ritual texts increases considerably, probably partly because of a general increase in written sources and partly because of very real ritual changes. We see the appearance of powerful thunder rituals to defeat a wide variety of demons. Judith Boltz has argued that these rites also made use of actual gunpowder, then a relatively new technology (Boltz, 1993: 274, 285–6). Gunpowder explosions in the early stages of developing firearms in China were used predominantly to scare horses and set fires, and of course firecrackers have long been used to drive away demons (compare

Franke, 1987). Firecrackers are called *baozhu*, which is written 爆竹 (exploding bamboo) with a character for *bao* that is closely related to the general term for violence discussed earlier. The use of gunpowder served to enact the power of thunder, which was widely thought to punish moral transgressions by slaying the perpetrator through lightning (Hammond, 1994; Li, 1981: 393: 3136–395: 3162). A strong case can be made that from the eleventh century onwards, more and more people had access to Daoist ritual expertise, with a crucial role for exorcist warfare on demons. The reasons for this are not well understood, although they are probably a combination of increased economic surplus allowing more people to pay for such expertise (and thus expanding job opportunities for professional ritual specialists) as well as improving education. Daoist ritual expertise presumed a certain level of literacy that would have been much less common in earlier periods (Davis, 2001: 14, 37, 293).

A random example from a Daoist ritual enlisting the Five Thunders lists the following terms: 'to behead and cut off the left ear' (*zhanguo* 斬馘; a traditional way of counting how many enemies a soldier had killed); 'to burn to death evil demons without leaving a trace' (*shaosha xiegui buliu zong* 燒殺邪鬼不留蹤); 'to behead evils and extinguish essences' (*zhanxie miejing* 斬邪滅精); 'to remove evil and attack temples' (*chuxie famiao* 除邪伐廟); 'to execute and behead the ten thousand evils' (*zhuzhan wanxie* 誅斬萬邪); 'to capture essences, abnormalities, evils and demons' (*zhuo jing guai xie gui* 捉精怪邪鬼); 'to tie them up' (*fu* 縛); and the list could be extended with further examples. In this particular ritual, thunder deities are enlisted who are so fierce that they need to be fed with 'bloody victuals' (*xueshi* 血食), i.e. the meat of freshly killed victims that still contains blood, in this case a red cockerel (*Daofa huiyuan*, 1986: 29: 440–3). As analysed by Edward Davis, the Daoist ritual specialist is supposed to use ritual means to visualize a divine general and thus become one with him, although he is not actually possessed and stays in personal control of the events (Davis, 2001: 49, 95–7).

Such demonological techniques were not the exclusive property of Daoist priests, although we are better informed about that particular group due to its higher level of literacy. The following account set in 1164 CE seems to concern a local ritual specialist who is best described as a shaman capable of speaking to the dead. We know of these events because they took place in the household living next to our informant. The wife of the neighbour was ill and the family invited a shaman (*wu* 巫, used here as a pejorative term) by the name of Shen Anzhi 沈安之 to 'put the demons right' (*zhigui* 治鬼). Our witnesses saw divine generals, dressed in martial clothes and several inches long, standing on the tea table. They ate, drank and talked like living beings. Through these Divine Generals (perhaps using a form of puppet theatre), the shaman was able to converse with a deceased concubine as well as the mother of the head of the family. Since the family of a son-in-law was plagued by monsters, they sent the same shaman to investigate. With the aid of his Divine Generals (*shenjiang* 神將) he arrested two monsters shaped like apes, but without hands and feet. Then he sent an army of several hundred soldiers equipped with crossbows to chase after a third monster.

> They also captured two people, one with a blue green headband and the other with its hair in two buns [like a girl], both their bodies covered with tree leaves. [The shaman] ordered them put in prison for a full investigation. They saw all of the hundred forms of horror in the under-world, such as the hot water cauldron and other instruments of torture. The demons were smashed to smithereens, but after they had died they would repeatedly come back to life. There was no mercy.
> (Hong, 1981: *bing* 1: 364–9)

Eventually, the shaman had a general capture a demon; the shaman person-ally broke all four of the demon's limbs, threw it into the air and caught it again on a sharpened stick. The demon submitted and confessed that he was a tree next to the house of the family, which would explain why the demons had been covered with leaves. The shaman cut open the demon's stomach and removed a rolled-up sheet of paper stating that this was the soul of this woman. When he put the soul back into the ill woman, she felt better the same night. The next day the Divine General reported that the demons had put up severe resistance, requiring an army of several tens of thousands of soldiers to combat them. The violence in this story is strikingly brutal, from the use of the Divine General with his huge armies to the cruel torture and complete destruction of the demons.

Exorcisms were part of a larger performative approach to issues that people encountered in their daily lives, whether it was an illness, possession or something else. Like any good healing process, a well-executed exorcism provided a context for the problem and perhaps even a solution. A crucial part were the struggles in which the ritual specialist was assisted by divine soldiers, but also the direct use of violence against demons that were resisting arrest and interrogation or continued to harass people (Davis, 2001: 102–7). Healing was imagined as a violent war in a very literal sense (Sivin, 2015).

Divine Soldiers making up divine armies could also be installed more directly in the local landscape, after an initial intervention by ritual specialists. Thanks to ethnographic fieldwork since the 1880s we are especially well informed about local beliefs in southern Fujian and the culturally closely related Taiwan. Here the divine armies are called Five Encampments (*wuying* 五營). Each army occupies a different direction (north, east, south, west and central) with its own colour and its own commander. Third Prince Li is in charge of the central yellow camp; he is a Divine General who is well attested since the twelfth century in ritual texts and local beliefs. The armies can be represented by the statues of their generals, but more commonly by coloured sheets, daggers or just sticks. These objects might also be placed around a village, providing permanent protection (ter Haar, 1998: 73; Jordan, 1972: 50–6, 130–3).

The belief in divine armies led by Divine Generals seems to have been connected to a major religious change that took place in the centuries after the fall of the Han dynasty in 220 CE. As we understand this particular religious change better, the following narrative will undoubtedly need further correction. The Daoist ritualist Lu Xiujing 陸修靖 (406–77) has left us the following account.

> Man and demon have mixed up. Stale energies from the Six Heavens have assumed official ranks and adopted titles. They have pulled together the hundred essences and the

Demons of the Five Types of Wounds (*wushang zhi gui* 五傷之鬼), dead generals of defeated armies and dead soldiers of armies in disarray. The men claim to be a General and women a Lady. They stand at the head of demon armies. Their armies travel around freely all over the world. They arrogate the dispensation of good fortune and censure people in order to get temples and residences. They request sacrifices from people and thereby put them in disarray, by making them butcher and kill their three types of animals. Their expenses run into the tens of thousands and they exhaust all of their savings and possessions. But they do not receive their protection and instead receive calamities from them, with uncountable numbers dying a wrongful death young and violently.

Lu Xiujing then continues to explain the Way of the Heavenly Masters as an approach to these cults, including their eradication through 'execution', 'punitive expedition', 'killing' and 'cleaning up'. His violent language against the religious developments of his day betrays a sense of frustration, and we now know that he was fighting a rear guard battle (Lu, 1986: 24: 779; Nickerson, 1996: 352; Von Glahn, 2004b: 64).

In his recent book Mark Meulenbeld has described the divine militarization of the Chinese landscape in great detail (Meulenbeld, 2015). From the eleventh century onwards prominent local cults were associated with military groups which took part in the processions of the deities and contributed to the building and upkeep of the temples. In later times local youngsters and/or riff-raff played the role of divine armies with gusto, using extensive make-up and adopting meaningful nicknames. We also read frequently of divine armies assisting these deities and when the worshippers of such cults travelled, their divine assistance travelled with them. They provided protection against bandits, but also against barbarian invaders (ter Haar, 2017: 24, 31, 68, 84, 95, 127–9, 170, 176, 200). Unlike the bureaucracy of the underworld or the pantheon summoned by Daoist priests, these local deities often had feudal titles such as emperor, king, marquis (ter Haar, 1995: 5–7).

As the attack by Lu Xiujing shows, the Heavenly Masters movement was originally fundamentally opposed to these local deities that originated in violently deceased generals and the like (Mollier, 1990: 128–9; Kleeman, 2016: 174–89). This is not surprising, since for much of this earlier period it was also an elite movement at some remove from peasant society. At the same time, Lu Xiujing used the same violent language and was clearly not fundamentally opposed to the use of violence. Here we should not forget that the different regimes that ruled during the Period of Disunion, Sui and Tang were extremely violent. Any change of ruler was usually accompanied by murderous infighting. When a much more open and mobile society developed from the eleventh century onwards, Daoist ritual experts could no longer count on the aristocratic elite to support them in a client–patron relationship, but had to start selling their expertise. They were forced to tolerate the deities that were worshipped by the same local communities (including its elites) who paid for their expensive rituals. While they did not approve of these deities, they could not reject or repress them, and the more prominent ones were incorporated in their rituals. Especially in southern China from the Yangzi region on, many deities originated in the kind of generals whom Lu Xiujing criticized. For reasons that are as yet unclear, they are much less common in the north, with the exception of the highly popular deities Lord Guan 關公 (also known as Emperor Guan 關帝) and Zhenwu 真武 or the True Martial One (Chao, 2011: 21–8, 57–8, 104–11; ter Haar, 2017: 36, 41, 83–5, 88, 95, 103, 134, 173–6, 178, 182, 197–200).

We have already seen that the early Heavenly Master movement conceptualized membership as becoming a 'Demon Soldier', allowing control over a small divine army that could protect against demonic attacks. In this early period the term 'demon' (*gui*) was still closer to its earlier meaning of 'dead person', and did not yet have the connotations of someone who had not made the proper transition to a new incarnation that it would acquire with the advent of Buddhism. Much later, the Yao, a local culture in southern China and the north of South-East Asia, would also initiate people into a ritual tradition that provided the ordained with his or her own divine army to fight against demonic attacks (Lemoine, 1982: 24–9). It seems likely that the Yao continued practices which were current elsewhere as well, but this has not yet been documented by secondary research.

The belief that divine armies also operated in the human world meant that these armies could be summoned to fight human enemies. This is precisely what deities like Lord Guan and Zhenwu were believed to do, driving away local bandits and border barbarians, as well as the demons of disease or flooding. The early anecdotal literature even claims that prominent generals were assisted by armies of Demon or Ghost Soldiers, including An Lushan 安禄山, the Tang general of Sogdian provenance who famously rebelled in 755 CE (Li, 1981: 76: 480; also 19: 129–1; 327: 2597–8; 369: 2935–7). The idea that rebel leaders were assisted by specialists capable of moving divine armies became a standard theme of vernacular literary traditions. Possibly, these were exceptional claims about extraordinary figures, but they again confirm the permeability of the human and the supernatural worlds, and how violence by divine armies could operate in both of them.

Later rebels and bandits (to stick to their labels in official historiography) sometimes selected titles that expressed violence or they adopted the names of Divine Generals summoned in exorcism (ter Haar, 2002a: 35–7). By assuming such nicknames, they absorbed the strong vital force connected to the name and became as violent and as powerful. I would also suggest that the seemingly random violence by these bandit-rebels derived from their self-perception as demonic forces with a licence to kill. The participation of real-life soldiers (well attested for the Song, Jin and Yuan) or martial arts troupes with theatrical make-up and armed with real or mock weapons (in later periods) as part of temple processions belongs in this same tradition. Their role is to protect the deity against demonic presences while on his way through the territory (Sutton, 2003: 126–55). It was also a pathway for local riffraff to be part of the festivities in supporting roles. Whether bandits, rebels or participants in a temple processions, the basic belief was the same, namely that Divine Soldiers could be impersonated by ordinary people in order to appropriate their violent power to fight demonic enemies. From this then derived a belief in invulnerability (Quan, 1991: *shang* 23–4).

The best-known example of local males defining themselves as an army of Divine Soldiers who are fighting demons are the Boxers of 1900. Although the concept of rebellion is problematic at the best of times, certainly in their early phase the Boxers were not seen as rebels by the

Qing state. More important, when seen from their own sparse text productions, they fought modernity as it was introduced in the form of Western inventions and very much supported the Qing. Crucial aspects of their activities were inspired by the demonological world view, beginning with the Boxer practice of referring to themselves with the term 'Divine Soldiers' (*shenbing*) (*Yihetuan shiliao, shang*, 5).

> The Jade Emperor is very angry because the Teachings of the Lord of Heaven (Roman Catholicism) and the Teachings of Jesus (Protestantism) do not respect the dharma of the Buddha. They cheat and destroy the saints and sages, as well as cheating and oppressing the soldiers and people of the Nation of the Middle (i.e. China). He has gathered up thunder and rain, and sent down 89,000,000 Divine Soldiers. The practice of the Fists of Righteousness and Harmony (*yihequan* 義和拳) was transmitted across the world. Divine power makes use of human power, to support and protect the Nation of the Middle, to transform people's hearts, and to eradicate the Westerners and their religion.
> (Shao, 2010: 148)

'Thunder and rain' served to scare away demonic enemies, as did the Divine Soldiers. They were the means with which Heaven would make sure that matters would be set right and that the proper order would be restored.

As Divine Soldiers, the Boxers deemed themselves invulnerable to bullets (*Yihetuan shiliao, shang*, 7). This acquires a further significance when we recall our discussion of firecrackers as a weapon of choice against demons. These were of course filled with gunpowder, but guns themselves too could be used exorcistically. I think that the belief in invulnerability was premised on the assumption that the Boxers were going to exorcise evil demons (Westerners in particular) and could therefore not be harmed by any exorcist weapons (the arms of Westerners, with which they were not very familiar anyhow). As one former Boxer put it many decades later, 'when they went into battle, a person would drink two mouthfuls of amulet-water and the leader would draw an amulet, he would draw an amulet on yellow paper. If one had been wounded, the leader would draw an amulet, the blood would flow fiercely, but when the amulet had been pasted on, they would go into battle' (Lu, 1980: 203). From a demonological perspective this view made good sense, even if transferring it to the human realm created a false sense of security.

The violence against real-life people, such as Western missionaries and their converts, and that against demons causing apocalyptic disasters was ultimately the same. One text expressed this quite literally: '[our weapons] will decapitate the evil demons (*xiemo* 邪魔) and kill the foreign devils (*yangyao* 洋妖); the [disasters of] weapons, water and fire that roam all over the place will be wiped clean together' (*Yihetuan shiliao, shang*, 9, but emending *xing* (star) to *xing* (to go, travel); also Lu, 1980: 205–8, 215). Thus it comes as no surprise that Boxers would be captured in possession of religious paraphernalia, including amulets (*Yihetuan shiliao, shang*, 284). This was not modern xenophobia but a much more traditional view in which the foreigners were part of a larger group of demons causing disasters, who could be successfully fought through the violent means of traditional exorcism. That their world view did not match the realities of the military world around them is quite another matter.

Besides the demonological world view there were also other approaches to problems of health and fear, although they rarely functioned in isolation of each other. During the Han dynasties, a theory-based Chinese medicine developed which saw itself as superior to the exorcist and strongly performative approach of demonology, but often incorporated parts of it in its daily practice. In the Buddhist world view the existence of demons, ghosts and deities was not denied, but the principal approach was to move these beings to a higher level by conversion and by accumulating moral capital on their behalf. A social change that is not yet well understood is how educated elites became less comfortable with the demonological world view over time, although it would be far too simplistic to dismiss this world view merely as 'popular culture'. Whether in person, or through intermediaries such as family members, educated male elites continued to take part in this culture.

Messianic and Millenarian Traditions

It is a long-established view in the field of Chinese studies that messianic and millenarian groups caused many violent events or even rebellions – a point of view derived from centuries of pejorative stereotyping of religious phenomena (ter Haar, 1992; Seiwert, 2003). There can be no doubt that some major rebellious events were connected to religious movements, although far more such events were not. The reverse is also true, since the large majority of religious activities, messianic or otherwise, did not lead to violent events. Here I use a fairly strict definition, in which groups and networks only qualify as messianic or millenarian if they have a well-defined expectation of an imminent end of times, preferably dated to a specific moment in the future.

The end of time will be accompanied by disasters, such as invasions by barbarians, demonic plagues, famine and drought etc. Many will die and only those who have prepared will survive. One approach to the end of times was Buddhist inspired, around the belief in the advent of Maitreya. When Buddhist missionaries began coming to China this belief manifested itself mostly as a distant expectation for all Buddhist believers. Later on this variant lost in popularity to the belief in an ideal Pure Land governed by the Buddha Amitābha. The messianic interpretation of Maitreya's future coming now became the dominant story about this bodhisattva. In this interpretation one could obtain election in his circle of chosen people by keeping a Buddhist lifestyle and the notion of a violent change of dynasty was absent (Zürcher, 1982: 12–16). Apart from this Buddhist approach, though at times in conjunction with it, there also existed a demonological messianic variant which was sometimes also associated with violent incidents and was often of a Daoist inspiration.

At the end of the Eastern Han dynasty two large-scale rebellions took place that both intended to put a new religious dispensation into place on the political level as well. They have shaped the way in which all successive political systems have looked at the power and dangers of religious culture. To many, the Han dynasty which had started its rule in 202 BCE must have seemed to rule forever, despite the short interval of the Xin dynasty. In the course of the first century CE, however, we start encountering beliefs in a new heavenly dispensation that would be governed by a new ruler (and, one assumes, ruling house). Usually the people making these claims were rounded up quickly, but the underlying prophecies and expectations continued to circulate (Seidel, 1969/1970). This development culminated in two rebellions in 184 CE with a strong religious background, namely the movement of the Heavenly Masters in Sichuan led by Zhang Lu 張魯 and the more diffuse movement of Great Peace or the Yellow Turbans (*huangjin* 黃巾) in eastern China led by Zhang Jue 張角 and others. The choice of the same year was no coincidence, since the next year corresponded to the *jiazi* 甲子 year, the first of the recurring cycle of sixty years and traditionally seen as a new beginning. Both movements tried to realize an ideal world on Earth, and they were forced to use violent means because the ruling Han dynasty had shown itself incapable of good government (Robinet, 1997: 53–74; Pregadio, 2008: 1156–7; Kleeman, 2016). We have no room to discuss the actual beliefs of these two movements, but their religious inspiration contributed to a long-lasting stereotype that organized religion might directly cause a violent rebellion (ter Haar, 1992: 48–55, 57, 163, 212–46, 282). The Yellow Turbans as a distinct movement were successfully defeated and disappeared again, although their practices may well have continued on a local level. The Heavenly Masters survived and out of their movement eventually grew a Daoist church that changed and evolved but that still exists today. It would often assist in the legitimation of imperial regimes (including the Tang, Song and Ming dynasties). Except in their early days, they were never directly associated with actual uprisings.

The stereotype that linked new religious movements to unrest and rebellion (often summarized as *luan* 亂 or chaos) proved very powerful, although it was not consistently applied. Whenever religious innovation took place, the established political and religious powers might feel threatened and attempt to suppress this innovation proactively, irrespective of whether the group in question had developed a violent dimension. In this logic state violence towards religion was almost unavoidable. In the late imperial period in particular the state developed a stereotyped view of alternative religious groups and networks, in which they were tainted with the brush of those rare cases in the past which had been actually co-inspired by religious practices and ideas. The default assumption from the mid-sixteenth century onwards was that the so-called White Lotus Teachings were behind whatever violent religious incident that the state imagined (ter Haar, 1992). This is not to say that religious ideas could not inspire certain types of violent events, although never in the simplistic and straightforward way that the stereotype presumed.

Once we ignore the stereotypes associated with the White Lotus Teachings label (or the connected labels for heresy, such as 'deviant' or *xie* 邪 and 'evil' or 'bewitching' or *yao* 妖), a different picture arises in which such groups (with stronger horizontal cohesion and shared collective practices) or networks (shaped like vertical lineages for the transmission of powerful lore) were only very rarely rebellious or violent. An example in point are the late imperial groups inspired by the myth of the Unborn Venerable Mother. According to this story, she had first banished immortals from Heaven to the human world because of their moral transgressions, but later sent down individuals to save mankind again because the end of time was nigh. Successive people would claim to be such saviours or their assistants, but these groups would never independently start violent incidents without additional inspiration. The belief eventually functioned as a background myth for networks that usually were quite different in nature, practising various simple techniques for imbibing cosmic stuff-energy (in the form of *qi*, which makes up everything in the universe) (ter Haar, 2019b). Only the messianic demonological paradigm did have the potential to develop into a violent and, from the perspective of the state, rebellious direction, even if it usually did not.

This paradigm stemmed from the overall demonological substrate of Chinese religious culture that I have already sketched out. The different versions of this paradigm all supposed that a leader would arise assisted by divine armies who could put an end to the demonological disasters that accompanied the end of time as we know it. It was not a big step for actual or prospective rulers to claim that they were this leader. Saviours in this paradigm would not claim to be an incarnation of Maitreya, following the Buddhist messianic paradigm, but descendants of former imperial houses or other great figures of the past. From the Han dynasty onwards it was quite common to claim descent from a Li figure, borrowing the charisma (~perceived attractiveness) of a figure like Laozi (who was believed to have the family name Li). After the fall of the Han, people also claimed to descend from the Liu family who had once ruled this mighty dynasty. Later on, family names such as Zhao (of the Song, who themselves claimed descent from the Yellow Emperor) and Zhu (of the Ming), but also Zhang (of the Heavenly Masters), were seen to have a special charisma (Wechsler, 1985; ter Haar, 1998: 254–5). Whenever later saviours claimed to have this kind of family connection, the imperial state usually took them for having rebellious intentions. The result was invariably violent repression.

People could obtain protection against the disasters of the end of time by following someone who claimed to be a saviour or have special access to him (they are nearly always men). In exchange people could receive the protection of his divine armies, represented in the form of amulets that one carries on the body or attaches to one's house. An early example can be found in a Daoist messianic text from the fifth century. It describes the end of the age as caused by corrupt government, causing flooding, failing crops, rebellions and so forth. Demonic armies will cause immensurable harm and illnesses. Copying this text will provide protection and will destroy these demons. According to this text, the Liu family of the former Han dynasty will again ascend the throne and the figure of Li Hong (a well-established saviour at the time) will appear again. Much of the actual text is devoted to the different ways of controlling and destroying the demons by means of banishing, tying up, killing, repressing (*jin* 禁), putting under oath, beheading, summoning or expelling (Mollier, 1990: 56–7, 60–1, 95–111; Von Glahn, 2004b: 63–4, 74–5). The crucial role of violence should be evident from this list. Even banishment or expulsion would have meant certain death in the violent wilderness outside human civilization. By initiation into a community of the elect, one could hope to escape these apocalyptic disasters (Zürcher, 1982). It seems that the elect did not themselves become Divine Soldiers or Generals, but did obtain the necessary ritual weaponry to fight the demons. This approach remained current in later demonological messianic traditions, but was also the basis of do-it-yourself ritual practice as well as the more elaborate rituals of exorcist specialists. In this particular text the good armies are called Heavenly Soldiers (*tianbing*) and their adversaries Demon Soldiers (*guibing*), but in most contexts this terminological distinction was not very clearly maintained.

Throughout the following centuries, people claimed the aforementioned illustrious family names, asserting that they were latter-day descendants of past imperial families. They would predict that the world was coming to an end at very specific dates in the near future, to be accompanied by demonic disasters and military violence. The claimants promised that they would be assisted by generals leading large armies of Divine Soldiers to restore the cosmic order. People would find protection by copying the scriptures with these prophecies and by drawing amulets and pasting them on the walls of their houses (ter Haar, 1998: 224–305). Amulets were essentially instructions to Divine Generals to enlist them with their armies in the struggle against demonic threats (ter Haar, 1998: 254–9). Since the cosmic order in these claims would be equal to the political order, the imperial system became nervous and overreacted.

Our understanding of the demonological messianic paradigm is distorted by the fact that we generally only learn about it in connection with a violent event, whether caused by state persecution or by the internal dynamic of the prophecies. A good example is the ten-century-old tradition of the *Sutra* (or *Amulets*) *of the Five Lords* (*wugongjing/fu* 五公經/符). It did tell of a violent end of times in years marked by the cyclical signs *yin* 寅 (associated with the tiger) and *mao* 卯 (associated with the hare), at which point a black wind will sweep everything away. At this point in time a Luminous King will appear and protect those who have acquired his amulets and/or copied his sutra. We can connect the text to various important and very violent moments in Chinese history, such as the fall of the Tang dynasty in 907 or the late Yuan rebellions in the 1350s. At the same time, there is also sufficient evidence from anecdotes and ethnographic reports, as well as prefaces and other para-textual information on extant manuscripts, that the text was simply used as a protective tool during moments of societal stress, moments that could indeed be defined as apocalyptic, such as the Boxer rebellion or the civil war of the 1940s (ter Haar, 2015). Because the scenario of a claim about the advent of a saviour assisted by divine generals sounded very real, both followers and the imperial state got confused and the latter often engaged in a wild goose chase for these generals (ter Haar, 2002b).

Because rebellions evidently are the most concrete form of violence that we can imagine from our contemporary, more or less secular point of view, we need to look in special detail at the most important examples of a possible association between religious rebellions and violence. Traditional historiography assumes that the co-occurrence of religious culture with violence in the form of a rebellion must mean that the latter was somehow caused by the former. It seems to me that this is a highly problematic approach. In traditional China religious practices were everywhere, and the Mandate of Heaven model of political legitimation meant that the entire political system was deeply religious and shaped by a broad repertoire of sacrificial and ritual practices directed at Heaven and its manifestations on Earth. We already saw how the Qin dynasty depicted the preceding age as one of unbridled violence (*bao*) and successive dynasties would make the same claim about the ruling house before them. The claim that a rebel leader was also a cosmic saviour was a stronger version of the assertion that the new ruler was going to bring order, but not fundamentally different. Some rulers even claimed to be such cosmic saviours themselves. This is also precisely why especially in the demonological messianic tradition Mandate of Heaven ideas are so strongly present (ter Haar, 1998: 306–24).

Some rebellions did make religious claims, but most did not. Even local protest did not necessarily adopt a religious guise and most of the time in most places religious culture remained eminently peaceful, despite the prominence of violence in the overall religious world view. Some rebellions did have a religious background and did make political claims, even though the underlying causes were to a large extent secular, such as natural disasters, foreign ('barbarian') threats, economic insecurity and so on. Two cases in point are the Red Turban rebellion that started in 1351 and the so-called White Lotus rebellion of 1622. Both rebellions were closely associated with the Grand Canal region, which was crucial in the provisioning of the capital in Beijing. The region was economically marginal and therefore inherently instable. Because of its crucial location, local rebellions here always attracted more attention than elsewhere.

We do not know whether the participants in the Red Turban rebellion from 1351 onwards chose their own name, since the historical information on their religious beliefs and practices is surprisingly limited given their impact on Chinese history. We do know that the rebellion borrowed elements from the demonological messianic paradigm, such as the belief in the Luminous King, the notion of disasters marking the end of time that will appear in specific years (in this case a *yin* 寅 year), and perhaps even the prominence of Nanjing (under the name Jinling) as a future capital. The belief in the support of divine armies led by an imperial descendant consisted of the idea of descent from the Song imperial family, the assistance of a divine general (supposedly from the late Northern and early Southern Song dynasties), and the support of 'excellent soldiers' from Japan. A special addition was the mention of Maitreya, although this element is not further developed in our sources. Even the explicit anti-foreign, or more specifically anti-Mongol, message of the rebels fitted in the demonological tradition, which saw barbarians as a major apocalyptic disaster. Their beliefs gave shape to enormous underlying social and economic tensions that had built up in the Grand Canal region due to earlier floods by the nearby Yellow River, harsh forced labour on repairing the Grand Canal itself and epidemics – perhaps bubonic plague (ter Haar, 2019a).

The so-called White Lotus rebellion of 1622 took place in roughly the same region. It was associated with a new religious movement headed by the Wang family and active since the late sixteenth century. The loosely integrated network was known under a variety of names at the time, and it is only contemporary officials who labelled it as White Lotus Teachings because of the putative connection between these teachings and rebellious activity (ter Haar, 1992: 227–38; on their autonyms, see Asai, 1990: 187–90, 292). By means of special meditation techniques one could make one's essence (*jing* 精), stuff-energy (*qi* 氣) and divinity (*shen* 神) coagulate inside the body, to produce cinnabar or the Golden Pill (*jindan* 金丹) which was then transported up through the body to the top of one's head or the Dark Gate (*xuanmen* 玄門). This would enable the practitioner to attain transcendence over life and death (Ma and Han, 1992: 613–32; Naquin, 1985: 266–7). Thus the movement also referred to itself as 'the transmission of the elixir of the single character' (*yizi danchuan* 一字丹傳) and various sources indicate the importance during transmission of the burning of incense. None of these practices was in any way exceptional at the time (Ma and Han, 1992: 595–6).

Xu Hongru 徐鴻儒 and other members from his network started a rebellion in 1622, not so much with the intention to spread their teachings as to create a form of alternative order. Or maybe they rebelled out of sheer desperation. Indeed, local tensions caused by flooding and droughts, combined with the economic exactions for the war against the Jurchen (later known as Manchus) in the north, were probably more important causes than messianic ideas (reanalysing Ma and Han, 1992: 569–70). Since all sources stem from the officials who put the rebellion down, it is difficult to know how important religious ideas were in the violent origins of the events. We do know that the leader of the Wang family network was not involved, even feigning illness after the events had broken out (Asai, 1990: 194–8). It must have been this lack of involvement that allowed large parts of the family network to survive the rebellion intact, allowing it to restart its religious activities and flourish into the late eighteenth and early nineteenth centuries (Ma and Han, 1992: 574–6). In his definitive work on the rebellion, Japanese historian Asai Motoi continues to see it as a Maitreyist rebellion, but also points out that actual evidence on this dimension is disappointingly small. Moreover, beliefs in Maitreya played no role in the original religious lore that was the core of the underlying religious movement. Notions of a change or restoration of the Mandate of Heaven may receive central mention in the sources related to the uprising itself, but originate in the widespread dynastic legitimation practices of the imperial era rather than the original religious message (Asai, 1990: 222–3, 236, 239, 292). Both in the Red Turban rebellion from 1351 onwards and the so-called White Lotus rebellion of 1622, external factors were much more important than the internal religious dynamic of the two movements.

During the Qing dynasty four of the larger rebellions had a clear religious background. These are the Wang Lun 王倫 rebellion of 1774, the so-called White Lotus rebellion of 1796–1804, the Eight Trigram rebellion of 1813 and the Heavenly Kingdom of Great Peace of 1851–64. We do not have enough room to discuss all of these in sufficient detail, so I focus on the White Lotus rebellion and the Heavenly Kingdom of Great Peace. In the case of the Wang Lun rebellion in the Grand Canal region of Shandong we have some idea of the religious ideas and practices involved. Nonetheless, Susan Naquin, the main Western historian of this short-lived rebellion, has pointed out that it is quite unclear how these ideas and practices led to the rebellion, since the actual events show very little shaping by religious ideas (Naquin, 1981: 37–61; Ma and Han, 1992: 1025–36). The Eight Trigrams (*bagua* 八卦) rebellion of 1813 in the northern plain is a very different example, in which beliefs about the approaching end of times motivated at least some of the participants. But even here, by no means would all new religious groups reached by its missionaries also take part in the rebellious events themselves (Naquin, 1981: 149). The rebellion was carefully planned, even though it had to spring into action ahead of time because it was being found out. It consisted of an attack on the Imperial Palace which was probably inspired by old beliefs in the existence of an urban sanctuary where one would be safe from apocalyptic disasters. In addition, followers elsewhere rebelled as well. The movement was suppressed within several months (Naquin, 1976).

The so-called White Lotus rebellion of 1796–1804 took place in the hilly regions of southern Shaanxi, Shanxi, Hubei and Sichuan. It did not call itself by this name and actually the participating groups did not primarily identify themselves on the basis of any religious ideas, but by the regional networks to which the participants belonged (Gaustad, 2000; ter Haar, 1992: 153). Because this time a large number of the religious figures spreading their oral lore and prophecies were arrested in the years before and during the rebellion, we have a much better sense of the role (and, more important, the non-role) these people played. None of the important teachers was involved in the rebellion or its preparations, even though they had been active for quite some time (ter Haar, 2019b). The rebellion itself was triggered by the ongoing state repression of prophecies in the demonological messianic paradigm that were circulating at the time. It was not a single rebellion with a central leadership in order to realize messianic aims, but a series of localized rebellions with very unclear aims. Indeed, it might be better understood as the collapse of central power, which had never been very strong in these marginal and mountainous regions.

In the previous few years, teachers had been travelling around telling stories about the advent of terrible apocalyptic disasters (such as military violence, floods and storms) and the need to obtain protection by reciting their mantras and following their saviours. Nothing was said on the need for violent action, whether to protect or to rebel, but the focus was always on the acquisition of a small body of oral lore. Although this lore was ultimately derived from shorter and longer written texts, it was always transmitted orally in the form of shorter or longer poems. This lore could then protect against whatever was coming. As such it was not that different from other forms of demonological beliefs, in which people would ascribe all kinds of attacks on one's health (mental and physical – although this is a modern Western distinction) to demonic activity. They would then acquire protective amulets or have rituals performed to avert these dangers and hopefully be healed. Since the Qing imperial state was particularly interested in the reconstruction of networks of teachers and pupils, already long before the actual outbreak of any violence, it spent much time on the identification of the saviours who were to appear and might be potential leaders. It did not spend much time and effort in investigating the actual impact of these figures on local people, because of its a priori assumption that any rebellion involving religious ideas must have been caused by these ideas, rather than by underlying socio-economic tensions or political repression. As it turned out, none of the teachers of demonological messianic prophecies had been directly involved in the rebellion at all (ter Haar, 1998: 224–305; Gaustad, 1994, 2000; Wang, 2014). When we look more closely at the real impetus for violent action, it turns out that it was really the local economic instabilities and the incessant search by the Qing state for a religious conspiracy that prompted resistance and local rebellion.

The ultimate religiously inspired rebellion of Chinese history was undoubtedly that of the Christian co-inspired Heavenly Kingdom of Great Peace. It was a violent and highly destructive rebellion, which was then put down with the usual extreme violence by the Qing state, lasting more than ten years. Identifying the mechanism by which the movement actually turned violent is not easy, but it is likely that its inspiration came from the demonological messianic paradigm, rather than from its specific brand of Christianity or the Confucian input about an ideal land system. The movement started with the vision in 1837 of an examination candidate of Hakka provenance, living to the north-east of Guangzhou (Canton). We know him today as Hong Xiuquan 洪秀全 (1814–64). In that year he had failed the exam for the third time and had a nervous breakdown (as we would label it). During his feverish dreams he visited God, was declared the younger brother of Jesus and received a mission to reform the world by ridding it of demons with a seal and a sword. It was only in 1843 that he started to interpret his earlier vision as a script for concrete action (for my own interpretation, see ter Haar, 2002a; classics are Wagner, 1982 and Weller, 1994; good on Hong is Spence, 1996; Reilly, 2004 again stresses the Christian dimension).

In their original interpretation, Hong Xiuquan and his close circle interpreted the demons primarily as Confucius, local deities and ancestors, which fitted surprisingly well with the iconoclastic views of the early Christian missionaries. Both the seal and the sword were not only classical objects of political and religious legitimation, but also powerful weapons against demons. This interpretation led them to destroy Confucian and Buddhist scriptures in their possession, as well as statues in village temples (Spence, 1996: 67–9). These acts of iconoclasm were violent attacks on religious as well as social life, given the fact that statues were seen as an essential part of the rituals and worshipping practices that kept the local community together. But it was not yet violence of the rebellious sort, indeed officials through the centuries engaged regularly in very similar acts of iconoclasm, destroying those statues and cults that they disapproved of. Hong and his close circle were now expelled from the county and journeyed to Guangzhou and then to Guangxi, to join distant Hakka relatives there and proselytize among them. Their earlier iconoclasm was now directed increasingly at the local cults of their enemies from other cultural and ethnic backgrounds. In the late 1840s two new members joined, Yang Xiuqing 楊秀清 (†1856) and Xiao Chaogui 蕭朝貴 (†1852), who changed the direction of the movement in important ways. In spirit medium sessions Yang claimed to be the voice of the Old Father (Jehovah or God) and Xiao the voice of Jesus, the Older Brother of Hong Xiuquan in his vision (Weller, 1994: 60–8; ter Haar, 2002a: 45). Their role would be extremely important in shaping the actual rebellion. Hong Xiuquan was never much of a leader, and depended in the early stages largely on his close collaborator Feng Yunshan 馮雲山 (1815–52). Yang and Xiao, and later others as well, introduced a crucial dynamism into the movement, since they could update the plans for the future thanks to their privileged access to God and Jesus themselves, who were evidently much higher in rank than Hong himself as the younger brother of Jesus.

Until Yang and Xiao joined the movement, its iconoclasm had been directed at cults in their native village (when still in Guangdong) and the cults of their local enemies (after they moved to Guangxi). Now the movement expanded its identification of the demons to include the Manchus, with obvious violent consequences. Under the increasing pressure of local Qing forces, but also inspired by the demonological paradigm, a plan was developed to move the entire movement to a holy city far away, Nanjing or the Heavenly Capital. The notion of a city like Nanjing as a safe haven is well established in Chinese messianic traditions, especially in their demonological versions. This also explains why they stayed there, rather than immediately moving north to deliver a final blow to a Qing regime that was shaking on its foundations. They retained their anti-demonic approach throughout, but in addition to the destruction of demonic cults the Taiping army would now also attack Manchu garrisons everywhere with a special vengeance (Wagner, 1982: 60–6, 74–5). In the end, they caused tremendous suffering, especially in the lower Yangzi region, but were finally defeated and eradicated in early 1864. Iconoclasm as such did not disappear, for with the advent of Christianity and later communism (itself highly indebted to Christian traditions of iconoclasm) the violent destruction of local cults and their icons, as well as all kinds of ritual experts, would reach a high tide. In the rebellion of the Heavenly Kingdom of Great Peace we see how the demonological paradigm could indeed be interpreted to legitimate extremely violent attacks on other ethnic groups, but at the same time this was quite a unique event.

The Enforcement of Norms and Social Values

Traditionally, the inhabitants of a village would be tied together by the worship of the God of Earth at an open-air altar and later also by more elaborate temple cults. They would engage in mutual help, but also social control. In all of this they were assisted by religious activities. On the whole we are better informed about the way in which the state tried to impose itself through taxes, local defence arrangements, laws and regulations. Since these are also easier to study for modern researchers, little attention has been paid to local informal arrangements for social control and the maintenance of local norms and values (but see Hsiao, 1960). The contribution of religious activities and beliefs towards maintaining local norms and values is surprisingly large, with a special role for violence as a fear and as a reality.

When local people created their own mutual agreements by swearing an oath, they would do so with supernatural witnesses who were expected to deliver violent sanctions upon anyone who transgressed the oath. This would then be expressed in the form of a special malediction as part of the oath, accompanied by animal sacrifice and sometimes another form of material destruction to symbolize the violence that would befall on the oath breaker(s) (Lewis, 1990: 43–50, 67–80; ter Haar, 1998: 151–218). The practice is well attested through the centuries, usually with slight adaptations to a changing religious environment. Thus, Emperor Wu (464–r. 502–49) of the Liang, famous for his support of Buddhism, swore an oath to abjure alcoholic drinks and meat. Despite the Buddhist injunction against violence, the oath included the vow (*yuan* 願) that if he should transgress the various dietary rules the assembly of great demons and deities would first punish him directly and then hand him over to King Yama in the underworld for all kinds of further suffering until all living beings have finally become Buddha's (Daoxuan, 664: 26: 298a).

In his extensive criticisms of what he perceived as distortions of Buddhist teachings and practices, the Yuan monk Pudu 普度 (1255–1330) inveighed against this same practice as follows:

> There are also stupid people who submit to the Buddha and take the vows, and then burn incense and swear their vows before the Three Treasures: 'If I break my vows, I will gladly have evil illnesses envelop my body and fall into hell eternally.' Or they say: 'May blood come out of my left eye and pus out of my right eye.' Their phraseology resembles that of documents in legal cases.
> (Yang, 1989: 116)

The same Pudu also wrote admiringly how the early Song Buddhist monk and ritual innovator Zunshi 'burned his finger and took an oath' to express the strength of his religious intentions (Yang, 1989: 82). There is a long tradition of sworn statements accompanied by a malediction, such as that described earlier by Pudu and especially well documented during the late imperial period. For example, the Triads from their origins in the late eighteenth century onwards would proclaim maledictions with some very violent threats to whoever would break the oath of mutual allegiance, such as 'may the Five Thunders Execute and Destroy us' (*wulei zhumie* 五雷誅滅) or 'may we die under the cuts of ten thousand knives' (*si zai wandao zhixia* 死在萬刀之下). They also re-enacted some of these punishments in theatrical form during the initiation ritual by executing the mythical traitor of their founding patriarchs (ter Haar, 1998: 151–223). These few examples should be enough to show that the practice of a violent threat towards oath breakers, including oneself, was a common practice across all religious approaches.

The comment by the Yuan monk Pudu suggests that in his time oaths containing violent maledictions may also have been practised in a legal context. On the basis of his much more extensive research, Paul Katz has suggested that there was no tradition of swearing an oath during this-worldly lawsuits (Katz, 2009a: 63–81, 116–78). If so, that would be a significant difference between divine justice and its earthly counterpart. Sworn oaths with violent maledictions were certainly practised initially during lawsuits in a colonial context such as Hong Kong, but this may also be because colonial officials were more open to popular legal customs and needed an equivalent to the Christian oath on the Bible (ter Haar, 1998: 164).

From the belief in a curse that would be carried out by the divine witnesses of an oath ceremony to appealing to divine forces for redress in case of an injustice was only a small step. Paul Katz has documented this practice in considerable detail. Usually, they would be deities who were capable of punishing transgressors in a suitably violent way, such as the City God or the Emperor of the Eastern Sacred Mountain (Katz, 2009a: 82–104, 116–78). In the mid-nineteenth century a devout worshipper of Lord Guan collected more than 100 similar stories from a single region within Xiangtan county in Hunan province, almost all of them dating from the years 1849–51. Lord Guan was of course well known for his impartial and righteous divine behaviour. Local people living in the surrounding of a local temple devoted to the deity put their complaints in oral form. The deity himself or his two loyal assistants then provided impartial and quite violent redress, in the form of painful illnesses that were often followed by death. People would feel terrible stabbing, fall into a coma, bleed profusely, be struck by lightning, develop swellings on the skin, become violently mad and so forth (ter Haar, 2013). It was important that there was a visible performance of violence, since otherwise the workings of divine justice would have remained unknown. People who were believed to have transgressed morally became physically ill or almost died, and local communities then interpreted this as divine justice. The belief in violent punishment was very real and the descriptions are very explicit about it.

The related belief that supernatural beings could play a role in the process of revenge as a form of punishment long antedates the rise of Buddhism or Daoism (Eberhard, 1967; Cohen, 1979). The third-century BCE 'Commentary of Zuo' (*zuozhuan* 左傳) contains the following example. In 536 BCE people of the state of Zheng dreamed that a former minister, who had died during violent political struggles a few years before, would return to take revenge on those who opposed him. When his intended victims actually died, the people (most likely urban elites) were even more scared than before and a panic followed that lasted many months. The unrest only stopped when a son of the former minister was given a high position again (Legge, 1872: 617–18). The belief that ghosts were capable of taking revenge was a direct extension of the importance of blood vengeance in Warring States society (and probably long before). This practice continued long after this period into the late Tang dynasty and then became less current as an acceptable elite practice, but not necessarily in local society (ter Haar, 2000). The more specific belief that ghosts with a grudge could avenge themselves already during someone's lifetime remained current throughout the imperial period.

Originally it was even feared that descendants could be punished for the misdeeds of their ancestors rather than for their own. This fear stemmed from the belief that one was never a single individual, but always an integral part of a larger kinship group. Benefits, as well as obligations and debts, belonged to the group as a whole and did not end with the death of a single individual. With the advent of Buddhism this changed. Guilt and punishment were now assigned increasingly on an individual basis, because of misdeeds in this life or during an earlier incarnation (Bokenkamp, 2007; Strickmann, 1981; Katz, 2009a: 28–33). The same was true for the fear of supernatural vengeance. In the following account from a late sixth-century collection of stories about vengeful ghosts, we learn of a man who had a son from his first marriage by the name of Iron Mortar. When the mother died, the man remarried. When his new wife gave birth to a son as well, she made a curse (*zhou* 咒, stronger than an oath): 'If you do not get rid of Iron Mortar, you are no son of mine!' She named him Iron Pestle, since the pestle pounds the mortar. From this moment onwards, she exerted herself to drive her stepson to death and with success. Just over ten days later, however, the ghost of Iron Mortar returned. He climbed on the bed of his stepmother and said: 'I am Iron Mortar. Although I was not guilty of the slightest crime, I was cruelly harmed and killed by you. My mother has put in a complaint to Heaven about our grievance and today we have obtained a warrant from the Offices of Heaven to come and fetch Iron Pestle. We will let Iron Pestle suffer from illness for the same length of time as I suffered. Since the time that he will leave the world is fixed, I will now stay here and wait for it.' Everybody in the house heard his voice as if he was back again. His stepmother 'kneeled and offered amends [for her deeds], slapped her face and presented sacrifices and libations to him'. None of this was to any avail and the ghost got even angrier. 'At the time Iron Pestle was six years old. When the ghost (or demon) arrived he became ill. His body hurt and his belly was bloated, he coughed so badly that he could not eat any more. The ghost repeatedly beat him and the places where he got beaten became blue and green spots.' After more than a month both the boy and his mother died, and the ghost disappeared (Li, 1981: 120: 842–3; Cohen, 1982: 45–7). Not every story was equally violent, but death and pain remain standard features of vengeance accounts throughout the centuries.

The following story of a rather brutal and violent redress of inequities begins in the chaotic years of the early Southern Song dynasty, around 1130 (Hong, 1981: *sanji* 3: 1324–5). A man of peasant stock made a career as a thief and robber, but each time he was found out he managed to escape, the last time by killing a prison guard. He changed his name and became a robber again, but this time he betrayed his companions, who were all executed. He now formed a loyalist army to support the dynasty, but after an exchange of 'words without foundation' he betrayed them and they were banished to the south. By contrast, he was rewarded with a position and made a successful career in the following years. Some people in his surroundings probably were aware of his previous activities, since this is how they then constructed the remarkable circumstances surrounding his violent death of many decades later.

> In 1195, towards the evening of each day one could see the vengeful demons circle around him, appearing and vanishing again indecisively. In the spring of the next year when he was sleeping during day time, he was beaten up with a whip by demons causing immeasurable pain. In the summer of that year several tens of strong fellows looking like people in an army platoon came straight to his residence, reproaching him: 'Your cruelty and lust for profit exceeded ferocious wolves. Our lot have all died innocently at your hands. As a result we were stranded at the Yellow Springs [as hungry ghosts], while you could wear proper clothes and hats, receiving emoluments in peace and quiet. Now we have put in a formal complaint as high as the Nine Heavens and as low as the Nine Underworlds. We want to make sure that you will leave and cannot linger on. Your descendants will be left without anything to chew on.' The entire household was stupefied by their words. Thereupon [the ghosts] together delivered a bastinado to him, making him bleed from his seven apertures whilst blaring like an ox. After several days he finally died. When he was buried in the wilderness, his coffin broke open and exposed his body to the open air. Pigs and dogs ate all of his flesh; they gnawed on his bones and left them everywhere. Although his three sons are still alive, he could not receive eternal sacrifices [since there was no corpse left].

The account spills over with violence and destruction. Many of these stories used the often violent way in which people might die in order to construct a satisfactory narrative vengeance on someone – and a high degree of violence to inflict pain and suffering was clearly an important part of it. Just dying was not enough.

This type of story with its strong legal structure and divine redress would remain current throughout the centuries. Most people would have known a similar event from their close surroundings. Explaining it away as fictional (which it would be from our own secular perspective) ignores the huge quantity of this material which suggests that it did have a strong appeal. The very real violence of death in a society without sedatives and without the now customary quarantining of terminal illness was made to serve an important narrative purpose, of satisfying people's urge for vengeance and comeuppance.

From the second century onwards, Buddhist missionaries then introduced new notions of a lasting underworld to China, in which one no longer just lingered on, but was judged and punished, before one was usually (but not always) reborn. It is this belief that transformed the notion of collective guilt as a kinship unit into the individual guilt of a single person (and his or her previous as well as future incarnations). This belief in an underworld fitted well with a much older practice of the confession of sins to be accompanied by appropriate and potentially violent self-chastising, such as beating one's breast, throwing oneself to the ground and knocking one's head on the ground, but potentially culminating with offering oneself up as a sacrifice in a self-burning ritual to obtain rain (Tsuchiya, 2002: 46–8; also see Meulenbeld, 2010). The practice of a confession during one's lifetime did not disappear, but given that sins might only become transparent after their death, post-mortem punishment was an important innovation next to the already existing possibility of post-mortem vengeance (compare Katz, 2009a: 28–42).

Historian and sociologist Wolfram Eberhard pointed out the importance of these beliefs long ago, but subsequent scholars have tended to ignore this dimension of the reproduction of social norms and values because of its religious or even 'superstitious' nature (Eberhard, 1967; Sawada, 1976). Originally, the Chinese underworld was merely a place where the dead resided, without much going on. That people believed in some sort of life after death is apparent from the contents of the graves of more prosperous people, as well as descriptions that set out an entire bureaucracy for the underworld (Poo, 1998: 167–77; Zhang, 2014: 106–19; Matsunaga, 1972). However unpleasant it might be without the right accoutrements, this world of the dead was not a place of punishment and looked in many ways like the human world.

Buddhism introduced the notion of an underworld as a location of passing justice before one could be reborn. This justice was carried out by means of extremely cruel, brutal and violent punishments. The violence of the underworld far exceeded that of the world of the living (Teiser, 1994: 1–15, and Timothy Brook in Brook, Bourgon and Blue, 2008: 122–51). Typically, the worst sinners were punished with considerable violence in the underworld, whereas lesser sinners were reborn in a lowly incarnation, often an animal that was then tortured or maltreated by humans. The notion of a judicial trial was a Chinese addition and stories about underworld justice became an important means for commenting on human society and its failings, such as corrupt judges and their underlings, judicial mistakes and so forth. At the same time, the belief in violent vengeance and karmic comeuppance remained prominent as well.

The following account from an early Buddhist miracle collection illustrates several forms of underworld violence (Li, 1981: 283: 2253–4; Zhang, 2014: 123–4, 129). The protagonist is Shu Li 舒禮, a 'shaman master' (*wushi* 巫師) who died of an illness in 322. Ordinarily, local people called him a Man of the Way, which suggests that he was a Daoist ritual specialist. The term 'shaman master' was used as a derogatory term for someone who evidently belonged to the ritual competition. After his death, the God of the Earth took him to the underworld for further processing. He was first taken to a pleasant area, but this turned out to be a mistake and he was handed over to a divine being with 'eight hands and four eyes, holding a bronze cudgel' who delivered him to Mount Tai, the traditional location of the Chinese underworld. The Prefectural Lord of Mount Tai then asked him what he had done during his lifetime.

Shu Li said: 'I served the 36,000 deities and performed exorcisms as well as sacrificial rites for people. Sometimes I killed oxen and calves, pigs and goats, and chicken as well as ducks.' The Prefectural Lord said: 'You killed living beings to flatter the deities, for this crime you need to be put on a hot grill.' He made a clerk take him to the grill. There he saw a creature with an ox head and human body, who grabbed an iron fork, pierced Shu Li and placed him on an iron bench. Turning from side to side, his body was scorched until it was fully burned. He begged to die, but was not allowed to. It lasted for one night and two days, and he went through excruciating bitterness. The Prefectural Lord asked the person in charge: 'Ought Shu Li's lifespan to be ended and should we take away his life in one go?' The other inspected the Record of Fate and found that he had a remaining lifespan of eight years. The Prefectural Lord said: 'Take hold of him.' The person with the ox head again pierced him on his iron fork and placed him beside the grill. The Prefectural Lord said: 'We now send you back to live out your remaining lifespan. Do not again kill living beings for licentious worship.' Suddenly Shu Li returned to live, but thereupon he stopped being a 'shaman master'.

Here the ritual practices of Shu Li are dismissed as 'violence' (more precisely as killing, which is prohibited by Buddhist rules) and he is punished by the infliction of extreme pain. When he returned to the world of the living, the pain had shown him the error of his ways.

Underworld beliefs now became a core part of Chinese religious culture. While we cannot measure the efficacy of these beliefs in enforcing social norms and values, we should realize that the same is true of the traditional legal system. Local magistrates might well draw on the support of local deities in making people confess to their crimes, for instance by having disputants take an oath in a temple or at least with a divine witness (Katz, 2009a: 53–9). Magistrates were also powerful supporters of local underworld cults, such as the City God and the Emperor of the Eastern

Sacred Mountain. The classical indigenous format of ten hells, each with its own king and some iconographical details, is already mentioned in a source from the late seventh century and becomes well attested by the ninth century, suggesting an increasing audience (Teiser, 1994: 78–9, 171–95, 196–219). Unlike the judicial system in the world of the living, judges in the underworld had several means at their disposal for obtaining the absolute truth about someone's life, in order to apportion the right incarnation and/or punishment. They had elaborate registers of good and bad deeds, although some stories suggest that these registers could be falsified and that mistakes were also made. Then there was the infallible Karma Mirror (*yejing* 業鏡 or *niejing* 孽鏡) in which King Yama showed people their past incarnations in order to explain their most recent fate in life. The judges also summoned witnesses from the world of the living to provide testimony. In this respect there was not much need for judicial torture, which was a fundamental difference from the magistrate's court in the world of the living (on the latter, see Dutton, 1992). Instead there was an abundant use of physical punishments and it is interesting to see how this was a major contribution by Buddhist culture that was carried from India to China.

Apart from personal narratives by or about people who had returned from the dead, graphic paintings and statues in temples and handwritten or printed descriptions also provided concrete information about the underworld and its role in enforcing social normal and values (Timothy Brook in Brook, Bourgon and Blue, 2008: 128–51). During the funerary rituals for the dead, ideas about the underworld were prominently displayed in the ritual paintings and enacted in short sketches in which the deceased travelled through the underworld and hopefully overcame the fates of punishment and rebirth, entering straight into the Pure Land of Amitābha (ter Haar, unpublished fieldwork during the 1990s). In the seventh month of the lunar year, rituals and plays were performed that involved visits to the underworld. The violent punishments that awaited sinners were an important part of the performance (Berezkin, 2017; Sedana and Foley, 2018).

In the cult of the Eastern Sacred Mountain that was extremely important from the Northern Song dynasty onwards several of these customs came together. The Eastern Sacred Mountain was the re-instantiation of Mount Tai from older religious beliefs and one of the main underworld cults of the later imperial period, as well as the supposed location of an important exorcist bureaucracy of Daoist-inspired ritual specialists. By the thirteenth century the bigger temples of this cult would have tens of little shrines as well, which contained offices devoted to parts of the legal and punitive process after death. Some of these tasks would have been familiar from a secular context, such as the arrest of the deceased and his or her transport to the underworld, but numerous offices were devoted to someone's past lives, karmic crimes and underworld punishment. Temples of this cult and other underworld cults were usually full of statues and wall paintings depicting the horrors of hell. In the temple of this cult in Beijing today we can still see the monstrous faces of the deities manning these offices and their assistants, as well as their rich repertoire of weapons and instruments of torture (Von Glahn, 2004a: 800–2; Swann Goodrich and Rinaker Ten Broeck, 1964).

As early as 1027, several regional officials in northern China complained that people took part in temple processions carrying military instruments made of wood, in addition to musical instruments and further paraphernalia reflecting the status of the deity. I have noted that deities were imagined as local rulers and therefore needed an armed guard in the form of divine soldiers to accompany them. Sometimes people carried the instruments of punishment during the procession, which served as a form of penance and reminds us of the ancient tradition of confession by self-chastisement (Xu, 1957: 165 *xingfa* 2: 21777: 16a–b (6503); 21777: 44a (6517); 19392: 111b (6551); 120b (6555); 129b (6560); 21779: 147a (6569); 158a (6574); Katz, 2009a: 107–8). Even deities might do some form of penance. Western observers have long been surprised by the fact that, during a period of extended drought, the statues of higher-order deities such as the City God were dragged through the dust. While they tended to see this as a form of coercion, we might also see it more plausibly as a form of doing penance by self-chastisement according to ancient tradition. During the same periods fasts were also very common, confirming this last interpretation (as coercion: Smith, 1899: 172; Hansen, 1990: 57; as contrition: Yu, 2012: 123).

In recent decades one could still pick up a detailed description of the underworld in many temples in Taiwan, which was called the *Jade Calendar* and had already been reprinted many times in the late imperial period. In essence this was an illustrated description of the underworld, provided with written explanations and depicting in great visual detail the punishments of the underworld. Disloyal men and women were impaled on a mound of knives; the heads of people who deceived and gave false testimony might be squashed in an iron grindstone or tied to scalding hot bronze pillars; others were boiled or frozen and so on (Timothy Brook in Brook, Bourgon and Blue, 2008: 128–51). Transgressions of the norms and values maintained by this religious system and by the secular legal system are well attested, but so are stories of people with remorse and people who get punished – at least in the eyes of others, when underworld punishment is concerned. We know that people worried considerably about their fate after death, and this resulted in devotional Buddhist practices as well as extensive rituals for the dead (de Groot, 1884; Watson and Rawski, 1988). Many of these rituals are still practised, so at some level those carrying these rituals out or paying for them still share in the old beliefs of a punitive and violent underworld.

The underworld was not just a mirror image of the world of the living. Narratives and customs around demons and ghosts were even more violent and more cruel, in order to convince and scare the living into following the appropriate norms and values. Similarly, these narratives and customs provided ironic and critical commentary, by speaking about underworld corruption and injustice or by allowing the living to get even with the unjust and powerful, at least after they had died. The violence in these narratives and customs fulfilled a powerful function on a variety of levels, serving both as a warning and as a source of satisfaction about the ultimate fate of people with perceived moral failings and transgressions.

Women could use the fear of demons or ghosts to take revenge, or to imagine oneself to take revenge, after they had committed suicide. This road was also open to men, but was especially powerful for women in light of their more limited repertoire for asserting themselves. Women might decide to dress in red clothes, which represented a heightened life force in imitation of the colour of blood. After they had committed suicide, they could return to haunt the living, whether their former husbands or other wives and concubines who had haunted them to death (Yu, 2012: 105–14). Like men, women could put in complaints before judicial deities such as the City God or the Emperor of the Eastern Sacred Mountain (Katz, 2009a: 100–3). A uniquely gendered practice was the Buddhist ritual of the Blood Pond, which is yet another example of the way in which Buddhist beliefs enlisted violence to support certain moral values. It was believed that women built up a karmic debt, because of their regular menstruation (assuming they were healthy and not underfed) and their massive blood loss during giving birth. As a result they would land in the Blood Pond Hell, which was precisely what its name indicated. Filial sons could then have special rituals performed to provide release from this terrible place (Grant and Idema, 2012).

From a present-day secular perspective, the different forms of religiously sanctioned agreements, oaths and vengeance, as well as beliefs about violent punishment during this life or in the underworld, may all seem quite powerless and insignificant. In a culture where the larger majority of people, different kinds of elites and ordinary people alike, believed in some form of rebirth and retribution, this type of divine enforcement of order will have been extremely powerful. Men had the additional possibility of going to court with the magistrate in the county capital, but in real life they too depended on informal village justice and divine justice as much as their women. One should not underestimate the power of local gossip and storytelling, and even ostracizing, in enforcing collective norms and taking narrative revenge on people who had transgressed these norms and their next of kin.

Sacrifice and Its Counter-Discourse

Sacrifice is the basis of Chinese interaction with the divine world, stretching back in time until we no longer have written sources and undoubtedly far beyond. Most beings in this world required alcoholic drinks and meat ('bloody victuals' as Terry Kleeman translated the core Chinese concept of *xueshi* 血食) and needed to be fed at regular intervals. The sacrifice was also very explicitly called 'the killing of [sacrificial] livestock' (*shasheng* 殺牲) or 'butchering [sacrificial] live-stock' (*zaisheng* 宰牲). In their sharing of meat and drinks, the gods were no different from ordinary human beings, who also constructed mutual bonds through sharing alcoholic drinks and meat. Once the divine beings had touched it, the meat and other sacrifices were prepared for a banquet that would be shared by all those who belonged to the community of worshippers; receiving one's cut of the sacrificial meat signified one's membership of the community. Animals would traditionally be killed just before the sacrifice, since their blood was an essential element of the sacrifice as it provided life force to the divine being. The animals which were offered up tended to be those which had been domesticated, from oxen (or buffalos), goats, sheep and pigs to dogs and poultry (both chicken and ducks). Differences in size and cost reflected differences in prestige. Some cults might specialize in specific animals, such as the famous cult of Shrine Mountain in eastern Zhejiang which preferred oxen, rather than the more common household pigs (Hansen, 1990: 148–52). Whereas local officials might reject local cults such as that of Shrine Mountain for their excessive sacrifices, they never rejected the larger principle of animal sacrifice. The animals were not killed with great care for their well-being, although for some animals a discourse about cruelty came into being over time. Nonetheless, the dominant indigenous discourse would not define this as violence.

The killing of living beings could not be performed randomly, except in war – whether between living beings or with demonic creatures. Because life and death were part of a larger cosmic process, even the execution of criminals had to take place in fixed places and at prescribed moments of the year, ideally in winter when nature was dead as well (Bodde and Morris, 1967: 45–8; Goossaert, 2005a: 36–7; Ho, 2000: 149–50). During droughts, any form of killing would be prohibited, allowing rituals for the advent of rain to bring back life to the crops and the human community to be carried out. This taboo applied to executions, but also to all killing of animals for food or sacrifice (ter Haar, 2017: 162).

Early in Chinese history (and in the prehistorical period) human sacri-fice, both voluntary and involuntary, was still quite common. In the Shang royal graves large numbers of beheaded human sacrifices have been found, their heads neatly arranged next to each other. A grave might also contain a small number of semi-voluntary male sacrifices, in a form of suicide for one's lord that would later be known as *xun* 殉. These people had also died by the sword, but they were not beheaded and were neatly laid out individually with grave gifts, although still within the royal pit as a whole and not next to it. The oracle bones from the Shang period confirm the importance of killing humans as a sacrificial practice, in great numbers and in a variety of ways, such as beheading, splitting the body into halves, dismemberment, beating to death, chopping to death, extracting blood, burying alive, drowning, burning to death, boiling and exposing the cut-open body to the sun in order to dry out. Different forms of killing were used for different purposes, and sometimes the victims were exclusively male or female. Inscriptions on oracle bones indicate that the victims had generally been obtained in battle (Wang, 2008).

While animal sacrifice has always remained a common practice, human sacrifice appears to have decreased considerably from the Zhou dynasty onwards, but precisely when it died out (and where) is still uncharted. Although there may have been religious reasons for this as well, the changing nature of society may also have been a factor. The Shang dynasty obtained its sacrificial victims and additional resources through military expeditions, but did not really conquer territories for its labour force. The Zhou seem to have engaged in a more stable relationship with other territories, in which resources could be extracted through a tributary relationship, without killing part of the labour force. By the latter half of the Zhou period, human sacrifice still happened at the altars for the Earth in the various feudal states that were fighting each other, but the victims tended to be leaders of the vanquished states, rather than ordinary prisoners of war (Kominami, 2009: 222–4). Since the surplus from a millet agricultural system is not very high, each farmer counted and excessive human sacrifice was wasteful. With the founding of a unified empire in 221 BCE, official human sacrifice went out of practice. This did not end violent infighting and political murder, but they no longer happened in a ritual context.

That human sacrifice was increasingly problematic also becomes visible in stories about communities living on the margins of the empire who still practised it – although it is not clear to what extent such reports are necessarily reliable descriptions of real customs or serve rhetorical purposes such as confirming the civilized nature of those who are telling these stories about the other. Some accounts tell of brave officials or individuals who made an end to human sacrifice, such as the story of Ximen Bao 西門豹 around 400 BCE who punished ritual specialists who sacrificed virgin women to the Lord of the River. He sent these specialists to be drowned in the river as a replacement sacrifice, with the aim of bringing the cult to an end. Since the story contains numerous Han dynasty details, it may not be a reliable account of the original events, but minimally suggests a growing rejection of such human sacrifice (Sima, 1959: 126: 3211–12; Lin, 2009: 417–19; Lai, 1990).

Daoist traditions practised rituals that enacted cosmic processes, which did not necessitate the sacrifice of meat. Their sacrifices were intended to be pure, consisting of rice and vegetables, since their supreme deities preferred that kind of food over bloody meat. Historically, some of them might eat dried meat, because of old it was the blood of fresh slaughter that was problematic and hurt the senses (Lavoix, 2002). On the whole, Daoist tradition apart from exorcist specialists rejected animal sacrifice and the use of animal products. From the Song dynasty onwards the dietary restrictions by Daoist priests were largely restricted to their ritual practice, but before that they were part of a special lifestyle in order to attain salvation. This distinction probably reproduces a general difference between Daoist practices before the Song dynasty and from that time onwards, with Daoism evolving from a personal ritual practice into a profession of providing ritual services (Pregadio, 2008: 167–9; Kleeman, 2016: 391–3).

With the advent of Buddhism came a radically different sacrificial approach, which had far-reaching consequences for Chinese religious practice because of the broad social impact of the teachings. In this respect Buddhist practice became the dominant counter-discourse of sacrificial practice. One of its core tenets was a prohibition on killing, in the belief that all animals are incarnations of former humans or might eventually incarnate into humans in a future life. There was a paradox here, since an animal existence was also a punishment for moral transgression in a human being's earlier incarnations. Being killed, whether by humans or by other animals, was part of the process whereby someone could work off his or her bad karma. Initially, the principal injunction was against taking part in killing or behaving in a way that might cause killing, but this only applied to monastics and did not at all mean the rejection of meat that was offered when begging for food. Laypeople only maintained a vegetarian lifestyle on specific days and/or for specific rituals, rejecting meat as well as alcoholic drinks. Buddhist monks attempted to extend the practice of not killing to the butchering of sacrificial animals in the worship of local cults, which is documented in several conversion accounts of local deities. In his oath to abjure alcoholic drinks and meat, already referred to, Emperor Wu of the Liang also included an elaborate instruction that local cults should no longer use meat sacrifices. He expressly mentions the cult of Jiang Ziwen, which was one of the most important cults in Nanjing, then the capital. In the long run, however, most cults continued to receive bloody meat sacrifices (Daoxuan, 664: 26: 297b; ter Haar, 2001: 130–2).

Unique to the Chinese situation is the spread of vegetarianism as a radical lifestyle among laypeople during the fifth century CE, and only after that also in a monastic context (Lavoix, 2002; Kieschnick, 2005). To embrace vegetarianism was a very radical step, given that sharing meat and alcoholic drinks was the mainstay of social as well as religious activities. To reject this severely impinged on one's communal and family life, unless everybody within one's network participated. Just how repugnant it was to mainstream society becomes evident from the fact that the main label against heretical groups from the twelfth to the fourteenth centuries was 'eating vegetables and serving the devils' (*chicai shimo* 喫菜事魔) (ter Haar, 1992: 48–55). Buddhist writers labelled lay Buddhists of the late Song dynasty 'vegetarians', intending it as a pejorative term (ter Haar, 2001: 133–4). Later as well, the lay Buddhist movement such as Non Action teachings, which originated in the second half of the sixteenth century in southern Zhejiang, suffered considerable social reprobation for its rejection of meat as well as alcoholic drinks (ter Haar, 2014: 96).

With the rejection of animal sacrifice also came stories about human cruelty to animals, whether for food or as sacrifice (Pu, 2014). The social history of Chinese views of violence towards animals still needs to be written, and here I can give only one brief example, from the Song period.

In our example, the mother of a local doctor loved eating crabs. She would buy a large number in the market during the crab season and place them in a big jar. Each time she wanted to eat a crab, she took one out and threw it into boiling water. When she died in 1141, her son organized a big ritual in a local Daoist temple, where the entire family attended. Only her ten-year -old grandson was able to see his grannie stand outside the door, bleeding all over her body. She told him that she was being punished for her habit of eating crabs. The family now had additional Daoist texts printed in order to gather more merit for a successful rebirth (Hong, 1981: *yi* 188–9). This story claimed to represent the grandson's point of view, but it was transmitted by adults and many similar stories have been preserved as well. At the same time, similar stories about killing the predominant sacrificial animal, the pig, are absent (Hong, 1981: *yi* 25: 314; *bing* 11: 457–8; *bing* 18: 514). Thus Buddhist-inspired stories about perceived cruelty towards animals did not generate a broader discourse against killing animals.

Stories about cruelty towards pigs and poultry are almost non-existent, which probably reflects the fact that the violent killing of these animals was essential to the performance of social and religious rituals. One interesting taboo did exist on the sacrifice and consumption of bovines, which was not of Buddhist origin, since they had a more general taboo on killing. Vincent Goossaert has documented this in great detail. The taboo on killing oxen went back to the Song period and had considerable currency especially among educated people. The ox traditionally constituted an important sacrifice, but it was also an important symbol of agricultural work as the principal draft animal in Chinese culture. The state tried to prohibit the killing of oxen since the Han dynasty, but with only limited success (Goossaert, 2005a).

By the twelfth century a full taboo on eating beef had finally come into being. It was seen as an impure custom but it was also associated with epidemic illnesses ascribed to demons punishing beef eaters (Goossaert, 2005a: 122–5, 2005b). One wonders if such stories might also hide the transmission of cow tuberculosis to humans, but this is for medical histor-ians to investigate. The taboo was not the result of Buddhist prohibitions, which extended to all animals, but arose among educated people of other religious backgrounds. It derives from the connection between agriculture and the ox, which became increasingly important during the Song dynasty, with the rise of an elite whose position was no longer based on warfare or connections to the imperial court in the capital, but on income from agriculture (Goossaert, 2005a: 160–206).

The much broader Buddhist discourse against killing included both the passive dimension of refraining from eating any meat (vegetarianism) and the active dimension of setting free life (*fangsheng* 放生). Most commonly the freed animals were small creatures such as fish that could be easily managed and much more rarely sacrificial animals such as pigs or chicken (Goossaert, 2005a: 63–4). With ups and downs the custom continued to be practised from the Song dynasty onwards and still exists today. Whereas setting free life was associated with Buddhism, the custom also stimulated a whole range of other charitable activities by educated elites according to the analysis of Johanna Handlin Smith, all intended to help fellow humans as well (Handlin Smith, 2009: 15–42). One of these activities was the development from the early Qing dynasty onwards of a discourse against the drowning of newborn girls as a method of birth control and the foundation of Nourishing Infants Halls with the aim of saving the lives of newborn children, most commonly girls (King, 2014).

Self-Inflicted Violence

China has a long tradition of religiously inspired auto-mutilation and suicide. In addition there are also strong traditions of largely secularly inspired auto-mutilation and suicide, which I leave out of consideration here except to note that every suicide created a ghost that might start preying on the living. I have already mentioned the self-sacrifice of officers of some status upon the death of their lord, in a practice called *xun* 殉, well attested in early China until the 200s BCE. Even more interesting is a northern tradition of voluntary exposure to the scorching sun, called *pu* and written with the same character as that for violence, *bao* 暴. In northern China where the summer sun easily reaches 40^0 Celsius for several months this would have been a potentially deadly ritual (Schafer, 1951: 130–3). This practice was combined with a penitentiary ritual of confessing to one's sins

(Tsuchiya, 2002: 48–9). The status of people performing this ritual could be quite high, ranging from the mythical King Tang in the sixteenth century BCE to emperors, high and low officials and Buddhist monks. By the twentieth century it was performed by local ritual specialists of low social status (Benn, 2007: 176–9; Schafer, 1951).

A second context in which violence to one's own body plays an important role is that of the martial medium, a type of possession specialist commonly found in southern China and best known from Fujianese culture. These specialists engaged in exorcist activities, to drive away a demon who was possessing someone and/or causing some kind of physical illness, or prophylactically to prevent demons from harming someone (de Groot, 1901: 1269–94; Elliot, 1955; DeBernardi, 2006). The weapons of the medium are not necessarily the same as in military contexts, because his violence expresses his life force and/or is intended to expel demonic beings. The medium's swords have specific adornments, such as the stars of the Northern Dipper, and in addition he may own exorcising whips, a prick ball for self-mortification and a halberd, as well as skewers to push through his cheeks or other parts of the body. In addition, he will sit on knife beds and ascend ladders of which the rungs are swords. Blood will flow abundantly. An experienced medium can be recognized from the scars on his body that result from this long-term practice of self-mortification. When asked, people claim that the mediums feel no pain and that this fact signifies the presence of the deity (Elliott, 1955: 52–8). Another possibility is that the blood or life energy turns him into an even more potent vessel of the divine voice, in the same way that people drink blood (usually not human, but that of a rooster) to empower their mouths when pronouncing an oath, or the application of human or animal blood to empower amulets and divine statues (ter Haar, 1998: 151–79).

We find examples of similar forms of self-mortification in ninth-century sources, with non-monastics imitating Buddhist forms of self-mutilation, such as cutting of their left arm, walking on elbows and knees, biting off fingers and cutting their hair, all of these in reverence of the Buddha's relic. In another instance they might burn their heads, scorch their arms and so forth as an offering to the Buddha (Kieschnick, 1997: 35–7). On one hand, such rituals can be taken as examples of the impact of Buddhist practices in which such self-mutilation was common, but at the same time they were probably fed by similar forms of self-mutilation by mediums as evidence of their divine possession.

For the Song period we also have detailed descriptions of spirit mediums, especially in connection with Daoist ritual practices, which have been studied by Edward Davis. Like their modern counterparts they performed feats of self-harm, in one example stepping on red-hot tiles and balancing a scalding hot iron cooking plate on the head, after which the divine general descended in the medium and the possession ritual continued (Hong, 1981: *zhijing* 5: 919; Davis, 2001: 146–7). According to a more general statement on twelfth-century spirit mediums, they can enter boiling water and fire (Hong, 1981: *zhiding* 3: 986, *zhiding* 4: 996; Davis, 2001: 149 and 292, note 95). The kind of violent self-mortification that we still find today on Taiwan and among Chinese communities in South-East Asia therefore probably has considerable historical depth. In Chan tradition, shouting and beating (which might escalate in beating up) were an integral part of the cultivated practice. We can dismiss these as non-violent, because we sympathize with the ultimate goals (as we perceive of them) of such practices, but it seems to me that they can still be conceived as violence of a sort. The beating easily developed into more excessive maltreatment (ter Haar, 2009: 448–50). The ritual importance of blood in providing life force to the mouth as a vessel for speaking oaths, as well as written charms and even statues and ancestral tablets, was taken up in the Buddhist practice of copying out sacred texts, such as sutras, with one's own blood (Yu, 2012: 37–61). This practice has considerable historical depth, but is still practised today under great admiration (personal observations, July 2016).

Buddhist tradition also practised its own extreme forms of auto-mutilation that horrified officials and other outside observers, but were surprisingly widely accepted within this tradition. Many of these practices can be connected to indigenous traditions, even though they did receive their own doctrinal and narrative rationalizations. Less is known as yet about similar practices in a Daoist context, but we do know that self-inflicted violence was practised there as well, for instance in the context of begging for donations to a religious institution (Goossaert, 2002: 77–133). Similarly, obtaining immortality through often highly poisonous medical substances yielding painful and violent deaths can be seen as a form of voluntary suicide from a non-Daoist perspective (Eskildsen, 1998: 92–3). We could treat these various customs directly within their larger indigenous context, but treating them separately helps us to appreciate that these forms of violence should not be dismissed as non-elite ('folk') customs, but were equally prominent if not more so among elite religious figures – defining elite in theological rather than sociological terms, in other words in terms of intellectual sophistication rather than in terms of social status.

Buddhist monks sometimes practised ritual exposure to the scorching sun to pray for rain, but also developed a more general practice of auto-cremation. It was legitimated in terms of the famous chapter of the *Lotus Sutra* in which the Bodhisattva Medicine King in a previous incarnation as Bodhisattva had doused himself in incense and oil, drank scented oil and wrapped his body in an oil-soaked cloth. Thereupon he made a powerful vow and sacrificed his body to the Buddha. He burned for 1,200 years and was then reborn (Benn, 2007: 58–69). Due to the popularity of this sutra, the briefest of references to it sufficed to provide orthodox Buddhist legitimation for the custom of auto-cremation (Benn, 2007: 69–77). I would add that like other forms of real or imagined violence (to use modern categories) it was also an extremely strong rhetorical statement meant to influence the audience into doing or letting go of certain things.

The practice could serve political aims – for instance as a form of protest – in China, but it is best known from Vietnam during the French colonial period and after (Miller, 2015; on the Tibetan case in the 2000s, see Whalen-Bridge, 2015). Equally, the violent nature of the act might serve to extend or renew the vitality of the Buddha's teachings and maybe even the world itself (Benn, 2007: 90–2). Violence is used here in very similar ways as in the tradition of uttering a rather violent malediction in connection with a sworn statement. Violence simply speaks more strongly than any verbal statements. Within the larger context of self-inflicted violence in Chinese culture, it was also not the anomaly that we might want it to be. Biographers came to terms with it, for instance by elaborating the political context of the event as support for the sangha. The prominent monk-intellectual Yongming Yanshou 永明延壽 (904–75) devoted a long treatise to the practice, arguing that it was a valid practice if carried out without any attachment to the body, in a completely empty manner, allowing the practitioner to transcend such worldly categories as right and wrong. Thus the right mental attitude was absolutely crucial (Benn, 2007: 104–31). Whether someone was seen to have the right attitude was ultimately dependent on the audience of the act and on subsequent historians.

Over the centuries, different degrees of self-burning continued to be practised (Benn, 2007: 127, 159–61, 197–8). When self-immolation was partial and only involved an arm or a finger, it served foremost to underline the resolve of the practitioner. In the cases discussed by Benn we find that burning a finger often marked a certain amount of recitation or other events, in a way similar to the burning of incense sticks to measure time (Benn, 2007: 40, 135–6, 149–51, 154–7). All forms of self-burning, like ordinary cremation, also produced relics that could then form the basis of devout worship by those left behind.

Another aspect of Buddhist practice that involved pain is that of burning incense in the form of little cones on top of the shaved head as part of ordination practice. After the ritual the scars remain as visible testimony. I am unable to trace its history properly, but it was common during the twentieth century and is still practised today, both on the mainland and in Taiwan (Welch, 1967: 298–300, 323–8). One can easily imagine that such a custom derives from more radical forms of auto-mutilation that have been incorporated in this more symbolic (but still quite painful) ritual form. Officially it is now forbidden on the mainland, but that has not stopped the practice, which shows how important such a lasting and public demonstration of faith through pain is to those who have undergone it.

Intrareligious Conflicts

Since Chinese religious traditions usually did not get enough room to develop strong institutions beyond the level of the local temple and monastery, China typically did not see the kind of violent conflict between different traditions that we know from Christian and Islamic traditions. As we have seen, this did not mean that violent incidents were entirely absent within Chinese religious traditions, including Buddhism and Daoism.

Messianic and millenarian prophecies sometimes did contribute to violent events, and even rebellions, although the role of state repression in triggering and escalating such events should not be overlooked. In addition there is a long history of civil strife and internal conquest, as well as invasions by and of others, indicating that the region as a whole was no less bellicose than others.

The Heavenly Kingdom of Great Peace, with its extreme iconoclasm against other religious traditions and eventually its identification of the demonic enemy as the Manchus, is one of the major exceptions in which a religious movement developed an internal dynamic that escalated into a violent rebellion against other forms of religion as well as the state. Although this movement was partially inspired by Christianity, I would identify its indigenous demonological dimension as an important cause for its violent development and certainly for the language that the movement adopted in this respect (ter Haar, 2002a). Christianity did become a contributing factor in other forms of violence, especially in the nineteenth century. During this century in particular, violent incidents frequently developed around local missionary stations. Some of these conflicts were religiously motivated, although this depends a bit on one's definition of religion. For one there was the attitude of the missionaries who were often so convinced of their religious and cultural superiority that they were incapable of seeing the other side. Reasons why indigenous communities protested might include land and control over other local resources, but also the feeling that their own religious culture was under threat. They were afraid that local missionaries used foundlings to harvest their eyes and organs in order to prepare an immortality medicine. They complained for instance that churches, especially their towers, damaged the local geomantic balance (*fengshui* 風水) and thereby caused misfortune to the community. When missionaries told their converts that they could no longer contribute to local rituals for rain, local communities felt that these converts were profiteers, since they would still profit from the success of such collective rituals. This created tensions that sometimes developed into violent attacks on Christian converts and their missionaries (Tiedemann, 2010; Bays, 2012). During the Boxer rebellion similar complaints also played a role, including the fear that missionaries were poisoning the water sources at a time when northern China was hit by one of its infamous droughts (ter Haar, 2006: 163–4, 171).

In my view, the repression of religious culture by the imperial state and its successors also belongs to the realm of religious conflict. The reasons for state repression did include socio-economic concerns, such as the fear in pre-Song regimes that bronze statues took too much bronze for coins out of circulation (Ch'en, 1956). But at the same time there were motivations that should be considered religious, for instance when the ruler and his advisors were also motivated by Daoist beliefs. Repression usually involved the defrocking of monks and confiscation of religious institutions for other purposes, rather than the killing of religious figures. Moreover, the persecutions usually did not last very long. Because of the stereotyping of mass religious movements as inherently tending towards rebellion, any group labelled as such could be persecuted. In practice, regular Buddhist and Daoist institutions, such as monasteries and properly ordained monks and priests, generally escaped such repression insofar as they were co-opted into a state bureaucracy for supervising religious life. New religious groups and networks did fall victim to incidental persecution, especially in the late imperial period and in the aftermath of religiously inspired rebellions. Buildings might be confiscated and leaders might be banished or executed, certainly when the event had escalated into local violence for whatever reason. On the whole, local officials tended to act in a measured way in order to preserve the social peace (ter Haar, 2014: 50–5, 60–2, 70, 74, 78–80, 155–6, 163, 182–8, 198–9, 204–9).

Another type of violence was directed by the state towards local cults. This type of destruction went much further than the incidental persecutions of Buddhism or Daoism, although the latter type of repression has received much more historiographical attention. Buddhist and Daoist monks or priests themselves might attack a single cult, describing it as demonic in nature. Early Daoist authors vehemently wrote polemical attacks against certain local cults that they felt were devoted to the 'stale energy' of deceased generals for a number of reasons, one of which was their practice of animal (i.e. blood) sacrifices. If they could, they had the buildings of the cult destroyed (Stein, 1979). At other times, they claimed to have converted the local deity into something more palatable or exorcised him or her much in the same way as Heavenly Master Zhang Jixian destroyed the snake demons in his massive exorcist battle in the early twelfth century (ter Haar, 2001: 130–2). Since the patrons of their rituals were often the same communities who worshipped these unpalatable local cults, in the long run Daoist or Buddhist priests had no choice but to find a peaceful form of coexistence with these cults through co-optation or by ignoring them.

Local officials felt less restrained by such considerations, although insufficient attention to the main local cults might cause bad relations between a magistrate and the local community as well. Over time, some of them engaged in the massive destruction of local cults and those ritual specialists who were outside the regular framework of state control of religion, such as shamans and mediums. Notorious (or famous among its supporters) is the destruction of hundreds of local shrines at the command of the Tang official Di Renjie 狄仁傑 in 688, which was just one example among many over the centuries. This kind of persecution did not just mean the material destruction of local shrines or temples, but disrupted the communal life which depended on these places. At the same time, local cults usually bounced back and adapted, because the suppression was rarely sustained for more than the duration of a single official's appointment (Hansen, 1990: 84–6; McMullen, 1993: 6–15; ter Haar, 1995: 15; Von Glahn, 2004b: 211, 237–41). Ritual specialists could go into hiding; shrines and temples could be rebuilt. This changed only in the twentieth century, when repression became annihilation. Restoration after 1976 has been very limited and can always be interrupted again by new and disruptive campaigns.

Officials also actively persecuted individual religious figures, especially mediums and shamans. I have already mentioned the famous case of Ximen Bao in ca. 400 BCE, who had the ritual specialists thrown into the river to drown instead of their sacrificial victims. In the following account from the late twelfth century, our source reports on a locally influential ritual specialist who was suppressed by the local magistrate. A battle developed between the specialist's ritual techniques and the magistrate's use of more conventional violence. He ordered the arrest of the 'shaman' (*wu* 巫, used here as a pejorative label) to have him bastinadoed. The shaman seemed not to care and left smiling after the beating. Soon after, the magistrate started to develop boils all over his face and only his eyes remained visible. This was seen as a counterattack by the 'shaman'. The magistrate now travelled personally to the house of the ritual specialist. There he had the man tied to a pillar and beaten up. All of the specialist's statues and scriptures were destroyed by fire. However, it was only after the magistrate and his officials had uncovered a secret cache of voodoo statues that they were finally able to break the man's power. The 'shaman' was again beaten up, until he had no more skin left. The face of the magistrate finally returned to its original state. The ritual specialist was drowned in the river (Hong, 1981: *bing* 20: 532). This type of repression continued into the twentieth century, and during mass campaigns against repression of local ritual specialists and members of new religious groups in the 1950s many were arrested, summarily executed or taken away to labour camps (Goossaert and Palmer, 2011: 146–50; ter Haar, 2014: 212–17). This kind of repression on behalf of the state could be labelled religious, since it was motivated by a competing kind of totalizing world view.

Despite the tensions that existed between different forms of religious expression, and the repressive behaviour of the state and its representatives, interreligious violence in the pre-modern period was limited, certainly when we take Western Christianity as our point of reference. I do not think this was because of any inherent tolerance of religious traditions in the Chinese case. There is enough evidence that these traditions would gladly get rid of their competition when given a chance. Instead the limited violence should be explained from the rather restricted institutional power of religious traditions above the local level, unless the imperial state took a more partial view in favour of a single tradition. What violence towards religion we do see is usually perpetrated by the state and its representatives. The imperial state did have strong views on right and wrong, for which an elaborate vocabulary was developed. And yet it was usually unwilling to estrange the local population by coming down too frequently and too harshly on 'licentious cults' (*yinci* 淫祠) or heterodox religious traditions (which could be labelled 'deviant' or *xie* 邪, 'evil' or *yao* 妖, and 'the sinister way' or *zuodao* 左道). When it did happen, it was either because of their supposed involvement in rebellion and/or because of the personal ideological concerns of the official(s) in question. In such cases the limited resources available for state action were all focused on repression, but invariably only for a restricted period of time, until another urgent matter called for attention. Otherwise social peace and the continued payment of taxes were the first priority of a successful local official.

Concluding Comments

One question that I have not addressed is to what extent the violent dimension of religious culture has stayed the same over time and whether its various forms of expression have now disappeared under the onslaught of modernization and state repression. Since I have personally witnessed many aspects of this culture in Hong Kong, Taiwan and Singapore, I am in no doubt that elements of this culture are still alive. The same is true of mainland China, although much less visibly so due to incidental campaigns and institutional repression, as well as of course the intense cultural change that results from economic development and globalization, as well as the increasing popularity of Christianity.

One major change over time was the advent of Buddhism, although not always towards a decrease in the use of violence. With it came strong beliefs about the extremely violent and cruel punishment of sinners in the underworld, and we also saw that Buddhists practised various forms of self-mortification. At the same time it is true that they opposed all forms of sacrificial killing for their own rituals, although the monastic tradition did not approve of the complete rejection of meat and alcoholic drinks or total vegetarianism by some lay Buddhist groups. Buddhist ritual specialists provided an alternative approach to dealing with demonic creatures and the deceased, who were not exorcised or destroyed as was the usual approach, but were provided with moral capital through ritual practice and even conversion to Buddhism. Especially important in this respect were funerary rituals, the Feeding of the Hungry Ghosts and the Gathering of Water and Land. Since Buddhist monasteries were never a strong political force, we rarely see them operate an independent military force either, but they were certainly not above the repression of competing religious approaches on a local level. Without the threat of violence in the afterlife,

Buddhism could not have succeeded. Moreover, individual practitioners made systematic use of different forms of self-mutilation in order to express their charismatic power, in the same way as might be done by traditional ritual specialists (such as shamans and mediums) and Daoist practitioners.

Within the scope of this Element I was not able to do justice to all aspects of the role of violence in Chinese religious culture. What I hope to have made clear is that the basis of Chinese religious culture, and with that many aspects of daily life, was the threat and fear of demonic attacks. These were inherently violent and could only be counteracted by violence as well – even if this reactive violence was masked by euphemisms such as execution, expulsion, exorcisms and so on. At the same time violence was a crucial dimension of the maintenance of norms and values, for instance in sworn agreements or in beliefs about underworld punishment. Violence was also an essential aspect of expressing respect through sacrificial gifts of meat (and in an earlier stage of Chinese culture also human flesh) and through a culture of auto-mutilation and ritual suicide.

Violence could play that role, as it does in our own cultures, because of its enormous non-verbal power. Using violence allowed someone to acquire control in very direct ways, for instance by beating someone up or even killing them, or alternatively by applying violence to one's body. This also worked in religious culture. But stories about violence, for instance about the demonic threat, the underworld and vengeance by the deceased, were equally powerful. Once memories of real events entered the same narrative structures as stories about the underworld or divine vengeance, these stories had very similar effects. The often excessive violence in these stories also made them especially tangible and expressive. I would argue that the violence that was common within the world of demons and the dead spilled over into the world of the living as well, especially at times of crisis. I have argued elsewhere that this was especially true in the twentieth century which was plagued by famine, droughts and flooding, civil war, foreign invasions and political campaigns. Only after the Cultural Revolution did some degree of normalcy set in with the economic reforms from the mid-1970s onwards. The violent way of interacting with opponents during the Speak Bitterness meetings during the Land Reforms of the early 1950s has strong resemblances to the tradition of putting a plaint of grievance before Heaven (in different forms, including Lord Guan or the City God). Farmers in that period would have been well acquainted with that tradition. Indeed, Mao Zedong himself grew up near a temple for Lord Guan that was locally famous for that very practice (ter Haar, 2013). Similarly, the parading of victims during the early Cultural Revolution resembles closely the parades of the City God and the Emperor of the Eastern Sacred Mountain, when self-perceived sinners would voluntarily carry instruments of physical punishment. With the collapse of the world view of the educated male elite, the violent viewpoint of the world that was so basic to the demonological substrate of Chinese culture came even more to the fore. It made accepting the militaristic world view of both the Nationalist and the Communist parties so much easier.

Bibliography

Asai, Motoi 浅井纪. (1990). *Min Shin jidai minkan shūkyō kessha no kenkyū* 明清时代民间宗教结社 の 研究. Tōkyō: Kenbun shuppan.

Bays, Daniel H. (2012). *A New History of Christianity in China*. Malden: Wiley-Blackwell.

Benn, James. (2007). *Burning for the Buddha: Self-Immolation in Chinese Buddhism*. Honolulu: University of Hawai'i Press.

Berezkin, Rostislav. (2017). *Many Faces of Mulian: The Precious Scrolls of Late Imperial China*. Seattle: University of Washington Press.

Bodde, Derk. (1975). *Festivals in Classical China: New Year and Other Annual Observances during the Han Dynasty, 206 B.C.–A.D. 220*. Princeton: Princeton University Press.

Bodde, Derk and Clarence Morris. (1967). *Law in Imperial China: Exemplified by 190 Ch'ing Dynasty Cases: With Historical, Social and Juridical Commentaries*. Cambridge, MA: Harvard University Press.

Bokenkamp, Stephen R. (2007). *Ancestors and Anxiety: Daoism and the Birth of Rebirth in China*. Berkeley: University of California Press.

Boltz, Judith. (1993). 'Not by the Seal of Office Alone: New Weapons in the Battle with the Supernatural', in Patricia Buckley Ebrey and Peter N. Gregory, eds., *Religion and Society in T'ang and Sung China*. Honolulu: University of Hawai'i Press, pp. 241–305.

Bourgon, Jérôme. (2003). 'Chinese Executions: Visualising Their Differences with European Supplices', *European Journal of East Asian Studies* 2.1, pp. 153–84.

Brook, Timothy, Jérôme Bourgon and Gregory Blue. (2008). *Death by a Thousand Cuts*. Cambridge, MA: Harvard University Press.

Burton-Rose, Daniel. (2018). 'The Literati-Official Victimization Narrative: Memorializing Donglin Martyrs in Eighteenth-Century Suzhou', *Journal of Religion and Violence* 6.1, pp. 106–26.

Ch'en, Kenneth. (1956). 'The Economic Background of the Hui-ch'ang Suppression of Buddhism', *Harvard Journal of Asiatic Studies* 19.1/2, pp. 67–105.

Chao, Shin-yi. (2011). *Daoist Ritual, State Religion, and Popular Practices: Zhenwu Worship from Song to Ming (960–1644)*. London: Routledge, 2011.

Cohen, Alvin P. (1979). 'Avenging Ghosts and Moral Judgment in Ancient Chinese Historiography: Three Examples from Shi-chi', in Sarah Allan and Alvin P. Cohen, eds., *Legend, Lore, and Religions in China: Essays in Honor of Wolfram Eberhard on His Seventieth Birthday*. San Francisco: Chinese Materials Center, pp. 97–108.

Cohen, Alvin P. (1982). *Tales of Vengeful Souls:* 冤魂志 *A Sixth Century Collection of Chinese Avenging Ghost Stories*. Taipei: Institut Ricci.

Daofa huiyuan 道法會元 (1986). In *Daozang* 道藏. Shanghai: Shanghai shudian; Beijing: Wenwu chubanshe; Tianjin: Tianjin guji chubanshe.

Daoxuan 道宣 (596–667) comp. (664). *Guang Hongming ji* 廣弘明集. In *Taishō daizōkyō* 大正新脩大藏經 (Vol. 52, 2103). Tōkyō: Daizō shuppan kabushiki kaisha, 1988 reprint.

Davis, Edward L. (2001). *Society and the Supernatural in Song China*. Honolulu: University of Hawai'i Press.

de Groot, Jan J. M. (1884). *Buddhist Masses for the Dead at Amoy*. Leiden: Brill.

de Groot, Jan J. M. (1901). *The Religious System of China*, Vol. VI. Leiden: Brill.

DeBernardi, Jean. (2006). *The Way That Lives in the Heart: Chinese Popular Religion and Spirit Mediums in Penang, Malaysia*. Stanford: Stanford University Press.

Dutton, Michael R. (1992). *Policing and Punishment in China: From Patriarchy to 'the People'*. Cambridge: Cambridge University Press.

Eberhard, Wolfram. (1967). *Guilt and Sin in Traditional China*. Berkeley: University of California Press.

Elliot, Allan. (1955). *Chinese Spirit-Medium Cults in Singapore*. London: London School of Economics and Political Science.

Eskildsen, Stephen. (1998). *Asceticism in Early Taoist Religion*. Albany: State University of New York Press.

Faure, David. (2007). *Emperor and Ancestor: State and Lineage in South China*. Stanford: Stanford University Press.

Franke, Herbert. (1987). *Studien und Texte zur Kriegsgeschichte der sudlichen Sungzeit*. Wiesbaden: Harrasowitz.

Gan, Bao 干寶 (fl. 315–36) (Wang, Shaoying 汪紹楹 ed.) (1979). *Soushenji*, 搜神記. Beijing: Zhonghua shuju.

Gaustad, Blaine Campbell. (1994). 'Religious Sectarianism and the State in Mid Qing China: Background to the White Lotus Uprising of 1796–1804'. University of California at Berkeley, PhD dissertation.

Gaustad, Blaine Campbell. (2000). 'Prophets and Pretenders: Inter-sect Competition in Qianlong China', *Late Imperial China* 21.1, pp. 1–40.

Goossaert, Vincent. (2002). 'Starved of Resources: Clerical Hunger and Enclosures in Nineteenth-Century China', *Harvard Journal of Asiatic Studies* 62.1, pp. 77–133.

Goossaert, Vincent. (2005a). *L'interdit du boeuf en Chine: agriculture, éthique et sacrifice*. Paris: Collège de France. Institut des hautes études chinoises.

Goossaert, Vincent. (2005b). 'The Beef Taboo and the Sacrificial Structure of Late Imperial Chinese Society', in Roel Sterckx, ed., *Of Tripod and Palate: Food, Politics, and Religion in Traditional China*. New York: Palgrave Macmillan, pp. 237–48.

Goossaert, Vincent and David A. Palmer. (2011). *The Religious Question in Modern China*. Chicago: University of Chicago Press.

Grant, Beata and Wilt L. Idema. (2012). *Escape from Blood Pond Hell: The Tales of Mulian and Woman Huang*. Seattle: University of Washington Press.

Hammond, Charles E. (1994). 'The Interpretation of Thunder', *The Journal of Asian Studies* 53.2, pp. 487–503.

Handlin Smith, Joanna. (2009). *The Art of Doing Good: Charity in Late Ming China*. Berkeley: University of California Press.

Hansen, Valerie. (1990). *Changing Gods in Medieval China, 1127–1276*. Princeton: Princeton University Press.

Harper, Donald. (1998). *Early Chinese Medical Literature: The Mawangdui Medical Manuscripts*. London: Kegan Paul International.

Ho, Virgil Kit-yiu. (2000). 'Butchering Fish and Executing Criminals: Public Executions and the Meanings of Violence in Late Imperial and Modern China', in Göran Aijmer and Jos Abbink, eds., *Meanings of Violence: A Cross Cultural Perspective*. Oxford: Berg, pp. 141–60.

Hong, Mai 洪邁 (1123–1202). (1981). *Yijan zhi* 夷堅志. Beijing: Zhonghua shuju.

Hsiao, Kung-chuan (Xiao Gongquan). (1960). *Rural China: Imperial Control in the Nineteenth Century*. Seattle: University of Washington Press.

Israel, George Lawrence. (2014). *Doing Good and Ridding Evil in Ming China: The Political Career of Wang Yangming*. Leiden: Brill.

Jordan, David K. (1972). *Gods, Ghosts, and Ancestors: The Folk Religion of a Taiwanese Village*. Berkeley: University of California Press.

Katz, Paul R. (2009a). *Divine Justice: Religion and the Development of Chinese Legal Culture*. London: Routledge.

Katz, Paul R. (2009b). 'Banner Worship and Human Sacrifice in Chinese Military History', in Perry Link, ed., *The Scholar's Mind: Essays in Honor of Frederick W. Mote*. Hong Kong: Chinese University Press; Shatin, pp. 207–27.

Kern, Martin. (2000). *The Stele Inscriptions of Ch'in Shih-huang: Text and Ritual in Early Chinese Imperial Representation*. New Haven: American Oriental Society.

Kieschnick, John. (1997). *The Eminent Monk: Buddhist Ideals in Medieval Chinese Hagiography*. Honolulu: University of Hawai'i Press.

Kieschnick, John. (2005). 'Buddhist Vegetarianism in China', in Roel Sterckx, ed. *Of Tripod and Palate: Food, Politics, and Religion in Traditional China*. New York: Palgrave Macmillan, pp. 186–212.

King, Michelle. (2014). *Between Birth and Death: Female Infanticide in Nineteenth-Century China*. Stanford: Stanford University Press.

Kleeman, Terry F. (1998). *Great Perfection: Religion and Ethnicity in a Chinese Millennial Kingdom*. Honolulu: University of Hawai'i Press.

Kleeman, Terry F. (2016). *Celestial Masters: History and Ritual in Early Daoist Communities*. Cambridge, MA: Harvard University Asia Center.

Kominami, Ichirô. (2009). 'Rituals for the Earth', in John Lagerwey and Marc Kalinowski, eds., *Early Chinese Religion*. Leiden: Brill, pp. 201–34.

Lagerwey, John. (1987). *Taoist Ritual in Chinese Society and History*. New York: MacMillan.

Lagerwey, John. (2010). *China: A Religious State*. Hong Kong: Hong Kong University Press.

Lai, Whalen. (1990). 'Looking for Mr. Ho Po: Unmasking the River God of Ancient China', *History of Religions* 29.4, pp. 335–50.

Lavoix, Valérie. (2002). 'La contribution des laïcs au végétarisme: croisades et polémiques en Chine du Sud autour de l'an 500', in Catherine Despeux, ed., *Bouddhisme et lettrés dans la Chine médiévale*, Paris, Louvain: Peeters, pp. 103–43.

Legge, James. (1872). *The Chinese Classics with a Translation, Critical and Exegetical Notes, Prolegomena, and Copious Indexes. Vol. 5: The Ch'un Ts'ew, with the Tso Chuen*, Part 1. London: Henry Frowde; London: Lane, Crawford & Company.

Lemoine, Jacques. (1982). *Yao Ceremonial Paintings*. Bangkok: White Lotus.

Lewis, Mark Edward. (1990). *Sanctioned Violence in Early China*. Albany: State University of New York Press.

Li, Fang 李昉 (925–96). (1981). *Taiping guangji* 太平廣記. Beijing: Zhonghua shuju.

Lin, Fu-shih. (1998). 'The Cult of Jiang Ziwen in Medieval China', *Cahiers d'Extrême-Asie* 10, pp. 357–75.

Lin, Fu-shih. (2009). 'The Image and Status of Shamans in Ancient China', in John Lagerwey and Marc Kalinowski, eds., *Early Chinese Religion Part One: Shang through Han (1250 BC–220 AD)*. Leiden: Brill, Vol. 1, pp. 397–458.

Lu, Xiujing 陸修靖 (1986). *Lu xiansheng daomen kelüe* 陸先生道門科略. In *Daozang* 道藏. Shanghai: Shanghai shudian; Beijing: Wenwu chubanshe; Tianjin: Tianjin guji chubanshe.

Lu, Yao 路遙 and others, eds. (1980). *Shandong yihetuan diaocha ziliao xuanbian* 山東義和團調查資料選編. Jinan: Qilu shushe.

Luo, Zhufeng 羅竹鳳 and others, eds. (1986). *Hanyu dacidian* 漢語大詞典. Shanghai: Shanghai cishu chubanshe.

Ma, Xisha 馬西沙 and Han Bingfang 韓秉方. (1992). *Zhongguo minjian zongjiaoshi* 中國民間宗教史. Shanghai: Shanghai renmin chubanshe.

Matsunaga, Daigan and Alicia Matsunaga. (1972). *The Buddhist Concept of Hell*. New York: Philosophical Library.

McMullen, David L. (1989). 'The Cult of Ch'i T'ai-kung and T'ang Attitudes to the Military', *T'ang Studies* 7, pp. 59–104.

McMullen, David L. (1993). 'The Real Judge Dee: Ti Jen-chieh and the T'ang Restoration of 705', *Asia Major Third Series* 6.1, pp. 1–81.

Meulenbeld, Mark R. E. (2010). 'From "Withered Wood" to "Dead Ashes": Burning Bodies, Metamorphosis, and the Ritual Production of Power', *Cahiers d'Extrême-Asie* 19, pp. 217–66.

Meulenbeld, Mark R. E. (2015). *Demonic Warfare: Daoism, Territorial Networks, and the History of a Ming Novel*. Honolulu: University of Hawai'i Press.

Miller, Edward C. (2015). 'Religious Revival and the Politics of Nation Building: Reinterpreting the 1963 "Buddhist Crisis" in South Vietnam', *Modern Asian Studies* 49.6, pp. 1903–62.

Mollier, Christine. (1990). *Une apocalypse taoiste du Ve siècle: le livre des incantations divines des grottes abyssales.* Paris: Collège de France, Mémoires de l'institut de hautes études chinoises.

Murphy, Andrew R., ed. (2011). *The Blackwell Companion to Religion and Violence.* Chichester; Malden: Wiley-Blackwell.

Naquin, Susan. (1976). *Millenarian Rebellion in China: The Eight Trigrams Rebellion of 1813.* New Haven: Yale University Press.

Naquin, Susan. (1981). *Shantung Rebellion: The Wang Lun Uprising of 1774.* New Haven: Yale University Press.

Naquin, Susan. (1985). 'The Transmission of White Lotus Sectarianism in Late Imperial China', in David Johnson, Andrew T. Nathan and Evelyn S. Rawski, eds., *Popular Culture in Late Imperial China.* Berkeley: University of California Press, pp. 255–91.

Nickerson, Peter. (1996). 'Abridged Codes of Master Lu for the Daoist Community', in Donald S. Lopez Jr, ed., *Religions of China in Practice.* Princeton: Princeton University Press, pp. 347–59.

Nickerson, Peter. (2002). 'Opening the Way: Exorcism, Travel, and Soteriology in Early Daoist Mortuary Practice and Its Antecedents', in Livia Kohn and Harold David Roth, eds., *Daoist Identity: History, Lineage, and Ritual.* Honolulu: University of Hawai'i Press, pp. 58–77.

Pinker, Steven. (2011). *The Better Angels of Our Nature: A History of Violence and Humanity.* London: Penguin.

Poo, Mu-chou (Pu, Muzhou). (1998). *In Search of Personal Welfare: A View of Ancient Chinese Religion.* Albany: State University of New York Press.

Pregadio, Fabrizio, ed. (2008). *The Encyclopedia of Taoism.* London: Routledge.

Pu, Chengzhong. (2014). *Ethical Treatment of Animals in Early Chinese Buddhism Beliefs and Practices.* Newcastle upon Tyne: Cambridge Scholars Publishing.

Qian, Yong 錢泳 (1759–1844). (1982). *Lüyuan conghua* 履園叢話. Taibei: Dali.

Quan, Heng 權衡 (fl. late Yuan–post 1371). (Ren Chongyue 任崇岳 comp.). (1991). *Gengshen waishi jianzheng* 庚申外史箋証. Zhengzhou: Zhongzhou guji chubanshe.

Reilly, Thomas H. (2004). *The Taiping Heavenly Kingdom: Rebellion and the Blasphemy of Empire*. Seattle: University of Washington Press.

Robinet, Isabelle (Phyllis Brooks, transl.). (1997). *Taoism: Growth of a Religion*. Stanford: Stanford University Press.

Sawada, Mizuho 澤田瑞穗. (1976). *Jigoku hen* 地獄變. Kyoto: Hōzōkan.

Sawada, Mizuho 澤田瑞穗. (1982). 'Konkaeru: kaisha heiyō no fōkuroa' 魂 かえる: 回煞避殃のフオオクロア, in Sawada, Mizuho, *Chūgoku no minkan shinkō* 中國の民間信仰. Tōkyō: Ōsakusha, pp. 406–50.

Sawada, Mizuho 澤田瑞穗. (1990). *Shūtei Kishu dangi: Chūgoku yūki no sekai* 修订 鬼趣 谈义: 中国 幽鬼 の 世界. Tōkyō: Hirakawa Shuppansha.

Schafer, Edward H. (1951). 'Ritual Exposure in Ancient China', *Harvard Journal of Asiatic Studies* 14, pp. 130–84.

Sedana, Nyoman and Kathy Foley. (2018). 'Ancestral Deliverance and Puppet Performance: Mulian Rescues His Mother and Bima Goes to Heaven', *Asian Theatre Journal* 35.1, pp. 85–98.

Seidel, Anna. (1969/1970). 'The Image of the Perfect Ruler in Early Taoist Messianism: Lao-tzu and Li Hung', *History of Religions* 9.2 and 3, pp. 216–47.

Seiwert, Hubert. (2003). *Popular Religious Movements and Heterodox Sects in Chinese History*. Leiden: Brill.

Shahar, Meir. (2008). *The Shaolin Monastery: History, Religion, and the Chinese Martial Arts*. Honolulu: University of Hawai'i Press.

Shao, Yong 邵雍 (2010). 'Yihetuan yundong zhong de daojiao xinyang' 義和團運動中的道教信仰, *Shehui kexue* 社會科學, 2010.3, pp. 144–50.

Sima, Qian 司馬遷 (fl. 100 BCE). (1959). *Shiji* 史記. Beijing: Zhonghua shuju.

Sivin, Nathan. (2015). *Health Care in Eleventh-century China*. Frankfurt: Springer.

Smith, Arthur H. (1899). *Village Life in China: A Study in Sociology*. Edinburgh: Oliphant, Anderson and Ferrier.

Soboslai, John. (2015). 'Violently Peaceful: Tibetan Self-Immolation and the Problem of the Non/Violence Binary', *Open Theology* 1, pp. 146–59.

Spence, Jonathan D. (1996). *God's Chinese Son: The Taiping Heavenly Kingdom of Hong Xiuquan*. New York and London: W. W. Norton & Company.

Stein, Rolf. (1979). 'Religious Taoism and Popular Religion from the Second to Seventh Centuries', in Holmes Welch and Anna Seidel, eds., *Facets of Taoism*. New Haven: Yale University Press, pp. 53–81.

Strickmann, Michel. (1981). *Le taoïsme du Mao Chan: Chronique d'une revelation*. Paris: Collège de France, Institut des hautes études chinoises.

Sutton, Donald S. (2003). *Steps of Perfection: Exorcistic Performers and Chinese Religion in Twentieth-Century Taiwan*. Cambridge, MA: Harvard University Asia Center.

Swann Goodrich, Anne and Janet Rinaker Ten Broeck. (1964). *The Peking Temple of the Eastern Peak: The Tung-yüeh Miao in Peking and Its Lore*. Nagoya: Monumenta Serica.

Teiser, Stephen F. (1994). *'The Scripture on the Ten Kings' and the Making of Purgatory in Medieval Chinese Buddhism*. Honolulu: University of Hawai'i Press.

ter Haar, Barend J. (1992). *The White Lotus Teachings in Chinese Religious History*. Leiden: Brill.

ter Haar, Barend J. (1995). 'Local Society and the Organization of Cults in Early Modern China: A Preliminary Study', *Studies in Central and East Asian Religions* 8, pp. 1–43.

ter Haar, Barend J. (1998). *The Ritual and Mythology of the Chinese Triads: Creating an Identity*. Leiden: Brill.

ter Haar, Barend J. (2000). 'Rethinking "Violence" in Chinese Culture', in Göran Aijmer and Jos Abbink, eds., *Meanings of Violence: A Cross Cultural Perspective*. Oxford: Berg, pp. 123–40.

ter Haar, Barend J. (2001). 'The Buddhist Option: Aspects of Religious Life in the Lower Yangzi Region from 1100–1340', *T'oung Pao* 87, pp. 92–152.

ter Haar, Barend J. (2002a). 'China's Inner Demons: The Political Impact of the Demonological Paradigm', in Woei Lien Chong, ed., *China's Great Proletarian Revolution: Master Narratives and Post-Mao Counternarratives*. Rowman & Littlefield: London, pp. 27–68.

ter Haar, Barend J. (2002b). 'Myth in the Shape of History: Elusive Triad Leaders', in Irene Lim, ed., *Chinese Triads: Perspectives and Histories, Identities, and Spheres of Impact*. Singapore: Singapore History Museum, pp. 19–31.

ter Haar, Barend J. (2006). *Telling Stories: Witchcraft and Scapegoating in Chinese History*. Leiden: Brill.

ter Haar, Barend J. (2009). 'Yongzheng and His Abbots', in Philip Clart and Paul Crowe, eds., *The People and the Dao: New Studies of Chinese Religions in Honour of Prof. Daniel L. Overmyer*. Sankt Augustin: Institut Monumenta Serica, pp. 435–77.

ter Haar, Barend J. (2013). 'Divine Violence to Uphold Moral Values: The Casebook of an Emperor Guan Temple in Hunan Province in 1851–1852', in Jeroen Duindam, Jill Harries, Caroline Humfress and Nimrod Hurvitz, eds., *Law and Empire*, Leiden: Brill, pp. 314–38.

ter Haar, Barend J. (2014). *Practicing Scripture: A Lay Buddhist Movement in Late Imperial China*. Honolulu: University of Hawai'i Press.

ter Haar, Barend J. (2015). 'The Sutra of the Five Lords: Manuscript and Oral Tradition', *Studies in Chinese Religions* 1.2, pp. 172–97.

ter Haar, Barend J. (2017). *Guan Yu: The Religious Afterlife of a Failed Hero*. Oxford: Oxford University Press.

ter Haar, Barend J. (2019a). 'Rumours and Prophecies: The Religious Background of the Late Yuan Rebellions', *Studies in Chinese Religions* 5.1, pp. 1–38.

ter Haar, Barend J. (2019b). 'Giving Believers Back Their Voice: Agency and Heresy in Late Imperial China', in Philip Clart and David Ownby, eds., *Text and Context in the Modern History of Chinese Religions: Redemptive Societies and Their Sacred Texts*. Leiden: Brill, forthcoming.

Tiedemann, R. G. (2010). *Handbook of Christianity in China. Vol. 2: 1800 to the Present*. Leiden: Brill.

Tsuchiya, Masaaki. (2002). 'Confession of Sins and Awareness of Self in the *Taiping jing*', in Livia Kohn and Harold D. Roth, eds., *Daoist Identity: History, Lineage, and Ritual*. Honolulu: University of Hawai'i Press, pp. 39–57.

Von Glahn, Richard. (2004a). 'Sociology of Local Religion in the Lake Tai Basin', in John Lagerwey, ed., *Religion and Chinese Society*. Hong Kong: Chinese University Press; Paris: École française d'Extrême-Orient, pp. 773–815.

Von Glahn, Richard. (2004b). *The Sinister Way: The Divine and the Demonic in Chinese Religious Culture*. Berkeley: University of California Press.

Wagner, Rudolf G. (1982). *Reenacting the Heavenly Vision: The Role of Religion in the Taiping Rebellion*. Berkeley: Institute of East Asian Studies, University of California.

Waley-Cohen, Joanna. (2006). *The Culture of War in China: Empire and the Military under the Qing Dynasty*. London: I. B. Tauris.

Wang, Ping. (2008). 'Methods of Killing Human Sacrifice in Shang-Dynasty Oracle-Bone Inscriptions', *minima sinica* 20.1, pp. 11–29.

Wang, Wensheng. (2014). *White Lotus Rebels and South China Pirates Crisis and Reform in the Qing Empire*. Cambridge, MA: Harvard University Press.

Watson, James and Evelyn S. Rawski, eds. (1988). *Death Ritual in Late Imperial and Modern China*. Berkeley: University of California Press.

Wechsler, Howard. (1985). *Offerings of Jade and Silk*. New Haven: Yale University Press.

Welch, Holmes. (1967). *The Practice of Chinese Buddhism, 1900–1950*. Cambridge, MA: Harvard University Press.

Weller, Robert. (1994). *Resistance, Chaos and Control in China: Taiping Rebels, Taiwanese Ghosts and Tiananmen*. Seattle: University of Washington Press.

Whalen-Bridge, John. (2015). *Tibet on Fire: Buddhism, Protest, and the Rhetoric of Self-Immolation*. New York, NY: Palgrave Macmillan.

Wyatt, Don J. (2011). 'Confucian Ethical Action and the Boundaries of Peace and War', in Andrew R. Murphy, ed., *The Blackwell Companion to Religion and Violence*. Chichester; Malden: Wiley-Blackwell, pp. 237–48.

Xu, Song 徐松 comp. (1957). *Song huiyao jigao* 宋會要輯稿. Beijing: Zhonghua shuju.

Yang, Ne 楊訥. (1989). *Yuandai Bailianjiao ziliao huibian* 元代白蓮教資料彙編. Beijing: Zhonghua shuju.

Yihetuan shiliao 義和團史料 (1982). Beijing: Zongguo shehui kexue chubanshe.

Yu, Jimmy. (2012). *Sanctity and Self-Inflicted Violence in Chinese Religions, 1500–1700*. Oxford; New York: Oxford University Press.

Yu, Yue 俞越 (1821–1907). (1986). *Youtai xianguan biji* 右台仙館筆記. Shanghai guji: Shanghai.

Zhang, Zhenjun. (2014). *Buddhism and Tales of the Supernatural in Early Medieval China: A Study of Liu Yiqing's (403–444) Youming lu*. Leiden: Brill.

Zürcher, Erik. (1982). '"Prince Moonlight": Messianism and Eschatology in Early Medieval Chinese Buddhism', *T'oung Pao* 68, pp. 1–59.

Cambridge Elements

Religion and Violence

James R. Lewis
University of Tromsø

James R. Lewis is Professor of Religious Studies at the University of Tromsø, Norway and the author and editor of a number of volumes, including *The Cambridge Companion to Religion and Terrorism*.

Margo Kitts
Hawai'i Pacific University

Margo Kitts edits the *Journal of Religion and Violence* and is Professor and Coordinator of Religious Studies and East-West Classical Studies at Hawai'i Pacific University in Honolulu.

❧

ABOUT THE SERIES

Violence motivated by religious beliefs has become all too common in the years since the 9/11 attacks. Not surprisingly, interest in the topic of religion and violence has grown substantially since then. This Elements series on Religion and Violence addresses this new, frontier topic in a series of ca. fifty individual Elements. Collectively, the volumes will examine a range of topics, including violence in major world religious traditions, theories of religion and violence, holy war, witch hunting, and human sacrifice, among others.

Cambridge Elements

Religion and Violence

Printed in the United States
By Bookmasters